Louisa May

THE WORLD AND WORKS OF
LOUISA MAY ALCOTT

Everyone knew the Alcott girls. Anna, quiet and proper, turned into an unexpectedly good dramatic actress whenever she set foot on stage. Lizzie was serene and cheerful, a born housekeeper whom her sisters called, "our little conscience." By the time May was four she was already a charmer with elegant airs. And Louisa—tall as a boy, thin as a beanpole, given to black moods and fits of inspiration—filled life with thunder and lightning and made it magic.

Louisa May

Louisa May

THE WORLD AND WORKS OF
LOUISA MAY ALCOTT

NORMA JOHNSTON

A BEECH TREE PAPERBACK BOOK
NEW YORK

The following are reproduced by permission of the Louisa May Alcott Memorial Association: portrait of Amos Bronson Alcott; photographs of Abigail May Alcott, Louisa May Alcott (c. 1850), Elizabeth Sewall Alcott, Anna Bronson Alcott, John Bridge Pratt, Louisa May Alcott (1860s), Frederick Alcott Pratt and John Sewall Pratt, and Louisa May Nieriker. Photographs of Louisa May Alcott at her desk in Orchard House bedroom, Abigail May Alcott in study of Orchard House, and Concord in the 1860s are reproduced by permission of the Concord Free Public Library.

Special thanks to Dr. Daniel Shealy, Assistant Professor of English, University of North Carolina at Charlotte, for his expert reading of the manuscript for this book.

Library of Congress Cataloging in Publication Data
Johnston, Norma Louisa May: The world and works
of Louisa May Alcott / Norma Johnston.   p. cm.
Originally published: New York: Four Winds Press. c1991.
1. Alcott, Louisa May, 1832–1888—Juvenile literature 2. Authors,
American—19th Century—Biography—Juvenile literature. [1. Alcott,
Louisa May, 1832–1888. 2. Authors, American. 3. Women—Biography.]
I. Title [PS1018.J64 1995] 813'.4—dc20 [B] 94-20624 CIP
ISBN 0-688-12696-0

1   3   5   7   9   10   8   6   4   2
First published in 1991 by Four Winds Press, Macmillan Publishing Company.
First Beech Tree Edition, 1995. Published by arrangement with
Macmillan Publishing Company.

For Madeleine L'Engle,
who makes "brave music"

Table of Contents

AUTHOR'S NOTE

1

THE YOUNG HOPER 1

2

". . . JUST THE FRIEND I NEEDED" 12

3

PASSIONATE PURITANS 20

4

". . . A CRASS CRYING BROWN BABY" 28

5

"I WILL KINDLE A FIRE FOR THE MIND" 36

6

"THIS IS THE WINTER OF MY DISCONTENT" 46

7

"THE NEWNESS" 55

8

THE CONSOCIATE FAMILY 62

9

"DIARIES OF A WILFUL CHILD" 73

10

"MY GIRLS SHALL HAVE TRADES" 86

11

"HALF-WRIT POEMS, STORIES WILD . . ." 97

12

"I'VE BEGUN TO *LIVE*" 108

13

"APPLE SLUMP" 121

14

"THE BLOOD OF THE MAYS IS UP!" 131

15

"THE AIR IS BAD ENOUGH TO BREED A PESTILENCE" 143

16

"FOR A FORTNIGHT I HARDLY ATE, SLEPT OR STIRRED" 150

17

LITTLE WOMEN 165

18

"*THE* MISS ALCOTT" 176

19

"HINTS OF A WOMAN EARLY OLD" 189

20

"A WOMAN IN A LONELY HOME" 202

21

"BRAVE MUSIC" 212

BOOKS FOR FURTHER READING 227

ACKNOWLEDGMENTS 231

INDEX 233

AUTHOR'S NOTE

I first met Meg, Jo, Beth, and Amy when I was six years old. I know, because I still have my copy of *The Christmas Book*, with its section called "Christmas with Little Women." I didn't know then that there was much more to the March—and Alcott—family story.

Two or three years later I found a copy of *Little Women* under the Christmas tree. It was like meeting old friends again and learning all the things I hadn't known about them. That feeling continued as I discovered all the rest of Louisa May Alcott's children's stories.

Like generations of readers, I grew up envying the March family everything but their poverty—their closeness, the way they never stayed angry, the way they always, *always* loved each other. As a young teen, I wept bitterly because I couldn't make my family as picture-perfect as the Marches, and resolved to be, like Louisa, a writer of books for girls.

I suspect that a lot of people—including myself—didn't recognize the strengths and affections in our own families when we were young because we were so busy longing for a *Little Women* kind of perfect family. I wrote my most popular books, the Keeping Days series, to pass on to readers what I had finally learned: that "family" has many different forms; that loving and liking don't necessarily go together; that you can love and hate the same person; and you can't necessarily love your relatives, at least not all the time.

Were Louisa May Alcott's own beliefs about family so different? For a long time she was regarded as "only" a children's book writer, or even a sentimental writer who was out of date. We read biographies of her and were dismayed to discover that she never even married a Mr. Bhaer, let alone a Laurie! Critics said she had never written a "real book" (meaning a masterpiece for adults) and regretted that she seemed to have wasted her life looking after her parents in a small town.

But this was before two women, Madeleine B. Stern and Leona Rostenberg, identified the thrillers and love stories Louisa wrote under pseudonyms. A trio of scholars, Daniel Shealy, Joel Myerson, and Madeleine B. Stern, began to edit and annotate for publication the private letters and journals of the Alcotts. As these became available to the public, we learned that Louisa May Alcott's family life had not been as picture-perfect as it had seemed.

Louisa May Alcott led a fascinating and complex life. In addition to being a writer in many different fields, she was an actress, an army nurse, an editor, a teacher, and a foster parent. She was an independent businesswoman, and in some ways acted as the mother—and father!—of her whole family, including her parents.

Louisa was a genuine American success story, a celebrity and heroine against tremendous odds. Personally, I admire her—and her writing, her optimism, and her courage—very much. My real appreciation of what she achieved, and how she was able to achieve it, came after I learned about her *whole* life (not just the *Little Women* part) and about her family.

Her father, Bronson Alcott, was a pioneer educator and philosopher who loved all children and adored his own. He would spend endless hours teaching them, playing with them, taking care of them. He was endlessly supportive of their dreams and talents. But he was also capable of putting his own philosophical beliefs before the well-being of his family. He couldn't—or wouldn't—earn a living to support them, and was subject to mood swings that came close to destroying him more than once.

Abba May Alcott, the mother Louisa immortalized as "Marmee," survived early tragedies to become a strong-willed, intelligent woman who passionately adored her husband even after she had lost all illusions about him, who fought everything and everyone to keep the family fed, clothed, housed, and together. Both parents, even at the worst of times, always respected their daughters' talents and encouraged them to follow their dreams. The Alcotts, in other words, were a dysfunctional family that achieved a miracle: They survived both as a loving family unit and as individuals of distinction, in spite of poverty, illness of body and mind, love and losses, and traumas that left lasting stress—all of which made its way, in one form or another, into Louisa's books.

At one time it was Bronson Alcott who was considered the genius of the family, and Louisa, the children's book writer, was looked on as "her father's daughter." I believe that she became what she was almost in spite of—not because of—the influence of her father. She was first and foremost "her mother's daughter"—Louisa May.

ONE

The Young Hoper

THERE ARE SOME PEOPLE who, although they may make wonderful grandparents, aunts or uncles, or teachers, should probably never be parents. They may love children. They may have a husband or wife whom they adore. They may long for the warmth, security, and affection of a home and family. But their most intense, most passionate, most fulfilling and all-consuming relationship is always the one between them and the visions and ideas in their own heads. Bronson Alcott was one of those people.

The man who would become Louisa May Alcott's father came from an old North of England family that had claim to greatness. The name Alcock (as it was originally spelled) was Saxon and meant "Little Hal." Thomas Alcocke of Silbertoth, Leicester, was granted a coat of arms some time around

1616. Its emblem was three cocks, and its motto was *semper vigilans*—"ever vigilant."

Thomas Alcocke and his brother George were among the group of Calvinist dissenters who sailed from Plymouth, England, in late March 1630. They landed at Dorchester Neck (now a part of Boston) at the end of May.

This was nearly ten years after the Pilgrims landed at Plymouth Rock. Both these groups of settlers were followers of the teachings of the reformer John Calvin. Both were Dissenters—that is, they disagreed with the preaching and practices of the Church of England. But there the similarity between them ended.

The Pilgrims of 1620 were Separatists. They believed in separating themselves totally from a church and people whom they thought were corrupt.

The settlers who arrived in 1630 were Puritans. They felt called to "purify" the church from within rather than separating themselves from it. They believed they must be "ever vigilant" of the purity of their community, their neighbors, their families, and themselves. Constant prayer, study of Scripture, and study of themselves were required. These religious beliefs were to have a profound effect on Bronson Alcott, and therefore on his daughter Louisa.

In time the Alcockes left Boston for Connecticut. In 1731, Bronson's great-grandfather John moved to a high point of land near what is now Wolcott, Connecticut, and named it Spindle Hill, because the area's main occupation was growing flax and spinning and weaving it into linen cloth. John did so well at Spindle Hill that when he died he left one thousand acres to be divided among his six children.

Those children divided it in turn among their children. By the time John's grandson Joseph Chatfield Alcox married

Anna Bronson, more than the spelling of their last name had changed.

On Friday, November 29, 1799, when Anna Bronson Alcox bore her first child and named him Amos Bronson for her father, the Joseph Alcox farm was only eighty acres of harsh, stony land. The unpainted house had been patched together out of two older buildings. It had three rooms, plus a loft where the children slept. The land was almost impossible to farm, but to young Amos Bronson's vivid imagination it was wildly beautiful.

Life on the farm was hard. Spinning mills were putting cottage weavers out of business. Two of the ten Alcox children died in childhood. There was little communication within the family. They were "Connecticut Yankees," much like their North-of-England forebears—tough-minded, practical, and scant of speech. But two Alcox family members were remarkable: the mother, Anna, and her son, Amos Bronson, who would later be known simply as Bronson Alcott.

Mrs. Alcox could scarcely read or write, but she came from a family that valued learning and she longed for the finer things in life. She passed both those passions on to her first and favorite child.

She taught her son Amos Bronson his letters by drawing them with a stick on the sand-covered floor of the house's keeping room. This was what we today would call a "family room" and was always the biggest room in the house. It was sure to have a fireplace (sometimes the only one in the house) for heat and cooking and some kind of "board," or table. This was where the family would eat—sometimes standing, sometimes very quickly, and often in almost total silence.

When Amos Bronson was six he went to a one-room

schoolhouse. It was only seven feet high, and twenty by twenty-two feet in length and width. The fireplace smoked in the winter, and the air was dank and suffocating in the summer.

Amos Bronson had only two friends. One was his cousin William Alcox, who lived down the road. The other was his mother. They were closer to each other than to anyone else. After he discovered his mother's journal, he began keeping one himself. First he had to make it, by sewing bits of paper together, with thin boards for a cover. He made his pen from a goose quill and his ink out of soot and vinegar.

He and William wrote letters back and forth to each other once a week, teaching themselves the elaborate writing style that educated people used in those days.

"Sir," Amos wrote to William, "Mankind wish to be considered reasonable human beings. . . . Opinions unsupported by reason, effect not its conclusion in investigating the truth."

A shining moment in Amos's young life came when his parents took him to visit his mother's brother, Tillotson Bronson, a magazine editor and school principal. In addition to other luxuries, Uncle Tillotson's home had a room all lined with books. To the boy who longed for learning, this was paradise. The room, the words, the very feel of the books were magical.

As soon as Amos Bronson was back home he shared with cousin William a wonderful dream. They would make a library of their own! By searching through all the Wolcott farms, the boys became the proud owners of some dozen donated books. Two became a part of Amos Bronson's heart and soul forever. One was Milton's epic poem *Paradise Lost*. The other was Bunyan's *Pilgrim's Progress*.

Many years later Amos Bronson wrote of the effect *Pilgrim's Progress* had had on him as a boy:

"This book is one of the few that gave me to myself. . . . How gladly did I seat myself, after the day's labours on the farm, in the chimney niche, with the tallow candle in my hand, and pore over its enchanting pages until late at night! That book was incorporated into the very substance of my youthful being. I thought and spoke through it."

It was no wonder. *Pilgrim's Progress* tells the story of how its hero, Christian, flees the Slough of Despond to reach the Palace Beautiful, then wanders through the Valley of Death until at last he comes to the Celestial City. For Amos Bronson, it was like looking into a mirror of his life—as it was and as he hoped it would one day be.

When Amos Bronson was thirteen, it seemed as though the dream were coming true. Uncle Tillotson took him into his own fine home and enrolled him in Cheshire Academy, the private boys' school where he was principal. Here was his chance to go on, as his uncle had, to Yale College and Divinity School.

He couldn't stick it out.

The boys at Cheshire Academy showed him, all too clearly, how "different" he was. His clothes were rumpled homespun instead of fine wool broadcloth. He spoke with a back-country dialect and accent—that is, when he spoke at all. He looked like a scarecrow and was treated as a scapegoat. After one month, he fled back to Spindle Hill, his formal education and his mother's dreams both at an end.

From then on he lived primarily in the world inside his head.

All his life, Amos Bronson Alcott was deeply moved by beauty, by sight and sound and touch. But he was also driven by a need to have things make logical sense. By the time he was in his middle teens, he was having trouble making the two sides of himself fit together.

One of the things he had the hardest time with was religion. For him the Puritan churches—Congregationalist, they were called by then—were very stark, although their stress on spiritual study and self-improvement made sense to him. When he was sixteen, he joined the Episcopalian Church. Episcopal worship and ritual was filled with color and poetry and music that must have appealed to Amos Bronson very strongly. But for him, something was missing in his new church also.

Then, when he was seventeen, he heard the famous Lyman Beecher, a Congregational pastor, preach at a revival service. In the spellbinding voice of Lyman Beecher, the Calvinist search for purity, self-improvement, and a New Jerusalem took on the emotional richness Amos Bronson craved.

But he was beginning to find more spiritual satisfaction in Nature than he did in being part of a congregation that worshiped God in church on Sunday. He believed that one could find oneself in Nature, and that in finding oneself one also found God. He didn't know it yet, but throughout America and Western Europe many men, especially artists, philosophers, and poets, were coming to the same belief. What he did know was that he was through with organized religion. He needed to follow his own inner light. He was also through with his old name. Now he signed himself, stylishly, *A. Bronson Alcott*. In his journal, he pledged himself to what he called "this chase after myself."

Unfortunately, he also had to chase after a livelihood. He worked in a clock factory, and he sold books door to door. Because he loved learning, he wanted to be a teacher. But he was so shy and reserved that no school board believed he'd be able to maintain discipline. In October 1818, filled with a deep

6

unrest, he boarded the sloop *Three Sisters* in New Haven harbor. He thought perhaps he might find a teaching post down south. It turned out to be, as he wrote in his journal, a "fool's errand."

His nineteenth birthday came while he was in Virginia. Christmas was coming, and peddlers were everywhere, hawking their wares to country people in town for holiday shopping. In the first half of the nineteenth century, the streets and byways of America were filled with these "gentlemen of the road" who traveled by wagon, by horse, or by foot with their peddlers' packs. They carried news of exciting happenings in the outside world, much the way television transmits news and popular culture today. Sometimes they farmed during the summers, but from harvest to spring planting they roamed the country, as far south as the Carolinas, with their needles and thimbles, sewing silk and bootstraps, children's toys and razors.

Bronson bought a set of almanacs from a Yankee peddler for three pence each. He sold them again for nine pence. Three hundred percent profit! This was richness! Bronson had—for the time being at least—found his career.

Over the next five years, Bronson made four long trips through the South. He covered many thousands of miles by foot, often in the worst of weathers. Once he was lost overnight in Virginia's great Dismal Swamp. The terror of that night came back to him in dreams all his life. Often he was seasick. Once he lay for a month nearly dying of typhoid fever. Cousin William was along on that trip, and he nursed him back to life. He came near death again in the James River when a drowning peddler clutched him in a stranglehold. He slept in the worst of places, and the best of places.

Many of the great aristocratic plantation owners of the South opened their homes and libraries to this reserved, scholarly young peddler. There Bronson saw for the first time the life he had only imagined but always longed for. It was a life of ease, elegance, and culture, and he was never to forget it.

It was also a life made possible only by the terrible institution of slavery. Somehow that truth never seemed to register on Bronson, even though he later became a leading antislavery crusader. More and more, during his peddling pilgrimages, he adopted the polished ways of his Virginia hosts.

He had left home in order to help his parents. He wrote a poem about how he meant to make them free from debt before he was twenty-one. He brought eighty dollars home from his first trip, and a hundred dollars from his second—princely sums in those days. But on the way home from his third trip his self-control broke.

While in New York, Bronson spent all his earnings on his first set of store-bought clothes—"black coat, and a white cravat of daintiest tie, crimped ruffles, gleaming amethystine pin . . . gold seals at watch-fob, jeweled watch within." Men were dandies in the 1820s, and Bronson, by now more than six feet tall, could wear clothes with an air. He had sowed his first wild oats.

His father had to pay the debts Bronson had left behind in Virginia, selling part of Spindle Hill to do so. Bronson simply couldn't manage money. He made two more peddling trips. Both were disasters, and by summer 1823 he was deeply in debt to his father.

His lack of success didn't bother him, but he was deeply disturbed to find himself *needing* money to meet his responsibilities. He felt that by being concerned about material things, he was no longer serving God. He vowed never again to make such a sacrifice.

8

He was penniless. He was far from achieving the glorious ambitions of his childhood. But he had learned a lot and changed a lot. He knew he could endure severe hardships, physical and mental, and survive. He knew that he was suited by nature to the peddler's life, which was in many ways like a pilgrimage. He knew that ideas mattered more to him than any of the material wonders in a peddler's pack. Moreover, in his travels he had discovered two things that were enormously important. He had a gift for teaching. And he had a gift of charm.

Bronson Alcott had found his life's work. He would be a peddler of ideas. He would share, especially with the young, all the wonderful things in books and in his own head. He would liberate people from the tyranny of soul-destroying old ways. All he had to do was find a place to do it.

Again Uncle Tillotson Bronson came through. Bronson became schoolmaster of Primary School #1 in Cheshire, Connecticut. And he immediately got himself into trouble.

In his enthusiasm he turned accepted notions of education upside down. He set up a school library of over a hundred books, which he somehow paid for himself. He garlanded the classroom with pine boughs and flowers. He taught geography by teaching map-making, arithmetic by counting beans and blocks. Reading was taught with pictures. Every child had a desk and a slate. All this seems very ordinary today, but in the 1820s it was unheard of. And Bronson sealed his doom by teaching both boys *and girls* gymnastics.

Overnight, he and his little country schoolhouse became famous. An article in the *Boston Recorder* proclaimed it "the best common school in the state—probably in the United States." Everyone liked what Bronson was doing, except the parents.

Rumors began to spread. This man was teaching dangerous ideas. Why did children need a library like that? Why couldn't they sit crowded together on backless benches the way their parents had? Why would any man buy books himself for other people's children? Why would any grown man encourage children to stay after school to discuss things with him, invite them to visit him at his home, *hug them sometimes?* It wasn't right for a teacher to become more important to children than their own parents! This man was a Pied Piper!

As with the peddling, Bronson's wonderful success ended with a crash. Another public school opened in Cheshire and drew away half of Bronson's students. Also, Cheshire Academy, which had been closed for a while, reopened. Worst of all, Uncle Tillotson died just as all this was beginning to happen, so Bronson was without any powerful support.

Bronson slunk back to Spindle Hill again, still in debt.

He couldn't know it, but his luck was about to change. Fifty miles away in Brooklyn, Connecticut, was a young Unitarian minister only two years older than himself named Samuel Joseph May. Like Bronson, he was a reformer. He was opposed to capital punishment, and he made his church the center of a universal antiwar movement. He preached against whiskey drinking. Then he set out to reform the Connecticut educational system.

Unlike Bronson, Samuel May knew how to do such things without setting off a revolt. As minister, he was a member of the local public school committee. He sent a broadside letter—what today would be called a flier—all over Connecticut, inviting people concerned about education to a convention to discuss how to improve the public schools.

It was the first convention of its kind to be held in the United States, and more than one hundred people showed up. Papers were read, educational philosophy was discussed. One of those papers was about the work of Bronson Alcott.

The ever-admiring Cousin William had written a letter about Bronson's success at the Cheshire school and sent it to Samuel May's conference.

That letter made a powerful impression on the young minister. He felt sure Bronson Alcott must be a genius, and immediately wrote Bronson an urgent invitation to come visit.

This was the public recognition that Bronson craved. He arrived on the parsonage doorstep on a late summer morning.

The Reverend Mr. May was not there to receive him. The lady of the house, Lucretia May, was upstairs recovering from the birth of her first child. So the parsonage door was opened for Bronson Alcott by the minister's sister and house-guest, Abigail May.

It was love at first sight for both of them.

TWO

"... Just the Friend I Needed"

THE MAYS OF MASSACHUSETTS AND CONNECTICUT were, like the Alcotts, an old New England family. But there the likenesses between them ended.

John May, a shipmaster from England, arrived in Massachusetts Bay Colony in 1640 with his wife and two sons. They settled in Roxbury, just outside of Boston. The name "May" was also spelled "Maies" or "Mayes" and comes from the Portuguese. It is also Jewish, and it's quite likely that Abba's original May ancestors were Portuguese Jews who took refuge in England during the Inquisition. Abba May, and her daughter Louisa, would inherit what was called the Mays' "Mediterranean look": olive skin, dark hair, and beautiful dark eyes that seemed rimmed with shadows.

Colonel Joseph May, Abba's father, had the family dark eyes and intense vitality. At twenty-one he founded a shipping company and was one of the richest men in Boston by the time he was thirty.

He had married with distinction. Dorothy Sewall was fifteen when she fell in love with the thirteen-year-old apprentice in her uncle's store. She waited for him for eleven years.

Joseph's bride was a member of the Puritan aristocracy. Her ancestor Samuel Sewall had been a judge at the Salem witchcraft trials of 1692 and had later publicly repented in church for his involvement; he was a pioneer believer in the rights of women and of Native Americans, and crusaded in print against slavery.

Dorothy Sewall May's aunt was the beautiful Dorothy Quincy who married John Hancock, first signer of the Declaration of Independence and first governor of Massachusetts. In 1827, still alive and twice widowed, Madame Hancock tyrannized over Boston society from her great house on Federal Street.

Colonel May, whose family had joined the new Unitarian church, believed deeply in the importance of looking after the welfare of other human beings. When he was young he devoted himself to making money, but when he was in his thirties something changed his life. A dishonest business partner used company money to invest in a land-speculation scheme, and the firm was forced into bankruptcy. Colonel May had had nothing to do with the dishonesty, but he felt honor bound to personally pay all the company's debts. He was so ashamed of the disgrace brought upon the family name that he suffered for a long time from severe depression. When he recovered, making money was no longer a goal. He spent the rest of his life in good works for the poor.

Colonel May never lost his love of culture and learning and beautiful things, nor his exuberance and love of life. His son Sam May remembered their home as always being cheerful.

Sam attended Harvard College and Harvard Divinity School. His sister Abba, the youngest of twelve children and her father's favorite, was very well educated for a woman of her time—much more educated than Bronson Alcott. Like most girls in her social position, she had attended a "Dame school" to learn reading, writing, and mathematics, and then had been given private lessons at home. These included painting, music, and a little French. At seventeen she had left home to study the humanities (French, Latin, history) and sciences (botany, chemistry, geometry, and astronomy) under a woman scholar. She began to dream of being a scholar herself.

At some time in her teens, Abba had become engaged to her cousin Samuel May Frothingham. He died suddenly while she was away. Abba was called home for the funeral and never returned to her studies.

Her life had already known tragedies. When she was six months old she had been badly burned on the face and the right hand. She was permanently scarred, with two of her fingers so contracted that she could never play the piano as she longed to. Six of her eleven brothers and sisters died in childhood, one of them terribly. Abba was only two when seven-year-old Edward, playing in the barn, accidentally impaled himself under his arm on a heavy pole and died before his mother's eyes. By the time Abba was a teenager, Mrs. May had become a chronic invalid.

When Abba was fifteen her eldest sister, Catherine Windship, died, leaving a son named Charles. Another sister, Elizabeth Willis, died and left two children. Brother Sam was already a minister in Brooklyn, Connecticut. Only Abba and her parents were left together in the family home on Federal Court.

The old charmed circle had been scattered, but the family closeness had not been broken. Because of Mrs. May's poor health, Abba acted as her father's hostess. She was, in the eyes of Boston, an "old maid," but a romantic one because she had "loved and lost." Abba's life was still a happy one.

Then, beginning in 1825, things happened that destroyed her family happiness forever. Her mother died, and a year later her father remarried.

The new Mrs. May was the widow of a former minister of King's Chapel, the Unitarian church the Mays attended. What's more, Mary Ann Cary May was only thirty-nine, a mere thirteen years older than her stepdaughter. She was very conscious of her position as the Reverend Cary's widow and Mr. May's wife. Now *she,* not Abba, was hostess and lady of the house on Federal Court. The atmosphere between the two women became a cold war.

Abba no longer had a home she could call her own. As an old maid of twenty-seven, she was unlikely to ever have one. Worst of all was that she knew from experience what a blessing a happy home could be. She had vivid memories of the May household as it once had been—of her father reciting psalms from memory, of music and dancing and reading aloud, of a door always open to visitors and a table always spread in hospitality.

Little by little Abba became, like many single women and childless widows of her time, a perpetual visitor in the home that had once been hers or in the homes of married relatives.

She could have become a scholar, or a writer. She had the gifts for either. Her letters, and the journal she kept all through her life, both show that. But she had what she herself regarded as a fatal flaw: she lacked mental self-discipline. Her mind wandered. She was given to moods, to fits of temper, and to depressions as deep as her happiness and optimism could be high. She wrote her brother Charles: "Tears fall, and fast, often betray my dissatisfaction and fail-

15

ure. I yield to despondency, rather than conquer by perseverance."

She must have been glad to escape to Connecticut and look after her dear Sam, his wife Lucretia, and the new baby, Joseph. Then one day at the end of that summer of 1827, Abba opened the door of her brother's white-frame parsonage and looked into the magnetic eyes of Amos Bronson Alcott.

For the rest of their lives, each of them was to remember the impact of that first meeting.

Bronson had never met a woman like Miss Abigail May.

No one would ever call her beautiful. She was tall and thick figured, in a time when daintiness and tiny waists were the feminine ideal. Her features were large, too, and not "regular." But she had a mass of dark chestnut hair, the beautiful dark eyes of her May ancestors, and a queenly elegance. Most of all, she had character, and a vitality that captivated people and made them overlook the scars of her childhood burns. No one who met Abba May ever forgot her. Dressed in silks or India muslins, in the bright light colors that were the summer fashion, she dazzled the young dreamer from Connecticut.

Bronson, too, made a striking first impression. He was very tall, with rugged features. His hair was a bright gold. He wore clothes well, although like many tall people he walked with a slight stoop. His head was generally tilted forward, as though his nose were perpetually in a book. His brows were heavy, intensifying this effect.

He had a way of giving a sudden, sideways look up at someone in an eager, shy, playful manner. Some people found this disconcerting or sly. Others, equally disconcerted, were enthralled. Abba certainly was. Bronson had inherited his mother's eyes, a strange light blue, intense and piercing. They were the eyes of a visionary—or a madman.

With uncharacteristic reserve, Abba recorded in her journal, "I found . . . an intelligent, philosophic modest man, whose reserved deportment authorized my showing many attentions. . . ."

"There was nothing of artifice, of affectation of manners; all was openness, simplicity, nature herself," was Bronson's reaction. "An interesting woman we had often portrayed in our imagination. In her we thought we saw its reality."

Bronson was a guest at the May parsonage for about a week. He and the Mays were very taken with each other. "This family is distinguished for their *urbanity,* and *benevolence*—their *native manners,* and *nobleness of souls—moral purity* and *general beneficences,*" Bronson wrote about them afterward. He added something remarkably revealing. "This May character which I so much love," he wrote, for once using *I* rather than his usual journalistic (or royal) *we.* This was personal. He was thinking of all the Mays, true, but especially of Abba.

The Mays were equally impressed. "A born sage and saint" was Sam's opinion. "[R]adical in all matters of reform, [Bronson] went to the root of all things. . . . I have never . . . been so immediately taken possession of by any man I have ever met in life."

For Bronson the days in Brooklyn went far too quickly. Sam and Bronson had many serious talks about the future of education in America. They discussed the idea of Bronson opening a school in Boston, possibly with the Scottish educator William Russell. Bronson had sent Russell an essay about the Cheshire school, and the Scotsman had published it in his *Journal of Education.*

In the afternoons and evenings the May parsonage rang with lively talk, with music, and with laughter, just as the colonel's house on Federal Court used to do. All the Mays were musical in some way. Abba was well known for her dancing, and she was a champion at chess. The card game of whist was also popular. Evening entertaining would end with a "collation," or refreshments of bread, cheese and apples, cakes, and tea.

Finally the time came for Bronson to board the stagecoach back to Wolcott. Sam and Abba stood in the parsonage doorway watching him cross the village green. Soon after, Abba confided to her journal that Bronson was "just the friend I needed."

She meant much more than "friend."

It took Bronson two months to write to Abba. We have no idea what was in his letter, but we do have her reply.

"Thank you, good Sir, for the kind remembrance you have manifested for Brooklyn female friends," she wrote. She told him that she'd often thought of writing him. "I am particularly pleased that you should have retained sufficient recollection of my identity . . . and can only regret the more that I did not ford the great gulf that heartless fashion and polar etiquette has made between us." She meant that well-brought-up young ladies weren't supposed to make the first move. But now that he *had* written—

Abba wrote on and on, the words "dropping off my pen so fast" that she was afraid her language was "incoherent" (it wasn't) and her writing a "shameful scrawl" (it was). She told Bronson that she was going to spend the winter at her brother's house and that she hoped to hear from him—and maybe see him—often.

Bronson didn't write anything about that letter in his journal. They corresponded all that fall and winter, and finally, three days before Christmas, he did confide to his journal, "Received a communication of an interesting nature from Brooklyn."

Abba's spontaneity, generosity, and admiration drew Bronson out of his introspective shell. He needed that, but he couldn't tell her so. It wasn't till he was in his eighties, well after Abba's death, that he put his passion for her on paper in poetry.

In that first letter, Abba told Bronson that if the Boston school materialized she hoped to be his assistant in it. Instead Bronson went to the mill town of Bristol, Connecticut, to teach in an elementary school. He began trying the same "enlightened" methods that had gotten him in trouble at the Cheshire school. They got him in trouble even faster here, and for the same reasons. By March 1828, he was again out of work. The failure gave Bronson the courage to leave small towns for the progressive atmosphere of a big city—Boston.

On his way, he stopped off for two days at the Brooklyn parsonage. It was ten months since he and Abba had last been together. They each pinned such high hopes on this meeting that, inevitably, it turned out a disaster. Both of them were afraid, insecure, and proud. Bronson, terrified by his depth of feeling, took refuge in cold silence. Abba was stunned—and what was worse, humiliated.

She told her diary that she was relieved to have been saved from "the overpowering influence of a more tender passion" and would henceforth avoid the man as much as possible.

Two weeks later she was back at her father's house in Boston. Given the way she felt about her stepmother, there was only one reason on earth that could have drawn her there.

THREE

Passionate Puritans

BOSTON ENERGIZED BRONSON. Thanks to Sam May he had letters of introduction to all sorts of influential people. Bronson was like a spinning top, rushing from meeting to lecture to dinner party, visiting bookstores, walking Boston's cobbled streets. It was a city in which old and new still coexisted in harmony.

Change was coming, but it had not yet come. The families in the old row houses and the outlying farms were still mostly descendants of the original Puritans. It was a city of prosperous merchants and small shopkeepers, of artisans and craftsmen, just as it had always been. Some people were very rich, but hardly anyone was very poor. Boston, in fact, was a boom town.

New ideas were booming, too, such as the romanticism of European poets and painters who gloried in Wild Nature and the Noble Savage. There were more radical ideas, too, such as abolition—the movement to abolish slavery. There were free blacks—or Negroes, as they were called then—in Boston. One, a merchant named David Walker, wrote an "Appeal to the Coloured Citizens of the World," proclaiming that "We must and shall be free. . . . America is as much our country as yours."

Boston's liberal thinkers applauded. Yet they, like Bronson, rarely connected the city's new wealth, and the ease and culture it made possible, with the slave labor that grew the cotton that supplied the northern textile mills.

Boston's most influential citizens, true to their Calvinist heritage, despised ostentation and the public display of wealth. They valued more the riches of mind and spirit. They were beginning to recognize the importance of early childhood education. They wanted a "nursery school," and the May family managed to get Bronson invited to become headmaster.

The committee's plan was for what is now called a preschool. It was to be a charity institution for the children of immigrants, most of them fleeing the Irish potato famine, who were beginning to arrive in Boston. Bronson thought he could get this first school on its feet in three months and then start another "to comprise the children of the more intelligent and more wealthy citizens where the means may be furnished of carrying our plans into more complete operation."

Abba had plans, too. The first was to make herself-Bronson's indispensable assistant.

Bronson was still acting strangely indifferent. But even so, gossip started. Who was this newcomer, this A. Bronson Alcott? The Reverend Samuel May was his main patron, and now the reverend's unmarried sister was dead set on becom-

AMOS BRONSON ALCOTT AT THE AGE OF FIFTY-THREE,
FROM AN 1852 PORTRAIT

ABIGAIL MAY ALCOTT (ABBA), C. 1860

ing the schoolmaster's assistant. What was going on? Abba hastily withdrew her application, muttering about "vicious slander."

Both Abba and Bronson were in a state of inner turmoil. Both of them were given to moods that seesawed between ecstatic highs and the depths of despair. Both were intensely emotional, though Bronson refused to face that fact about himself. Abba shut herself up in the Federal Court house for weeks, afraid of running into him if she went out. Bronson poured his own confusion out in his ever-present journal. He wrote, as usual, with elaborate, formal language, but his confusion and inner conflict were real.

He wanted to be a solitary pilgrim, free to live in the world of his own mind. He also wanted a home, the kind he'd never had. "How long shall we exist, but to know that we but *half* exist?" he wrote.

Finally Bronson made the first move. He wrote a note to Abba and delivered it to her *in person* at the home of her sister, Louisa Greele. A few days later, he gave Abba his journal with some passages marked for her to read.

Fortunately, Abba was able to read between the lines. She saw that Bronson did love her—passionately. And that he had no idea she was in love with him.

The big move was up to her—and she made it. After taking a walk with him, during which she lost her nerve, she invited him to call on her at her sister's house. There she told him she loved him, and that he could either cherish or reject her.

Bronson didn't know how to handle this. At last, when Abba's suspense must have been unbearable, he pulled out his journal and showed her some passages she *hadn't* seen.

They told her everything she needed to know. That night she wrote ecstatically to her brother Sam, "I am engaged to

Mr. Alcott not in a school, but in the solemn—the momentous capacity of friend and wife. . . ."

Abba immediately started taking care of Bronson. She asked Sam to try to get Bronson's salary raised.

Bronson was living in a boardinghouse on Charles Street, not far from Federal Court. Boardinghouses were safe and respectable, and for a certain sum per week a "paying guest" also received a place at the "board," or family dining table. Apartments, as we know them today, did not exist.

Abba often joined Bronson at the Charles Street dinner table, or he joined her at the colonel's house or at Louisa Greele's home in Brookline. As Abba's fiancé, accepted into the May family, Bronson began to bloom. His journal entries became less stilted, and he dropped the "royal 'we.' " Abba was his "dear A!" She called him "Rasselas," for a fictional prince who roamed the earth looking for the meaning of existence. He was, he wrote, as happy as he could bear to be.

Then tragedy again struck the May family. In November 1828, Louisa Greele died, leaving two small children. One month later Sam May's little boy, Joseph, died. Abba, who adored children, was grief-stricken. Bronson didn't know how to comfort her. Louisa's husband wasn't able to take care of his children, so Abba would have to do so. Since Abba and her stepmother were at swords' points, Abba and the orphans would have to move in with Sam and Lucretia.

The fact that Abba was engaged to be married made no difference. A *married* woman's first duty was to her husband and her children. An *unmarried* woman's duty lay with her birth family. Engagements often had to be broken, or postponed for years, because of this. Things would have been different if only Bronson had had enough income to marry Abba immediately, but he didn't. He had left his post at the charity school and started a private school for boys, but he was deep in debt. In April 1829, Abba had to leave Boston.

Bronson consoled himself by mapping out a series of topics for their correspondence. But letters didn't comfort him for long. His father died, and he went back to Spindle Hill for the funeral. He still couldn't pay that old debt he'd owed his father, but he gave up his share in the Alcox farm. Then he left Spindle Hill forever.

Letters from Abba stopped coming. In June he heard from mutual friends that she was ill. For a week he was nearly out of his mind with worry. In Connecticut, Abba was pining in a depression, the ailment she was prone to all her life.

Suddenly Bronson was galvanized into action. It was always like that—once an idea possessed him, he could not rest till he put it into action. The idea was to *marry Abba*. He knew now that he could not live without her.

Bronson the peddler went out to make the most important sale of his life, to the most crucial customer: Colonel Joseph May.

It wasn't easy. While the colonel shared many ideals and goals with Bronson, he deplored Bronson's impracticality. He particularly disapproved of Bronson's idea that working for a living was something to be scorned. He was also hurt that neither Bronson nor Abba had asked his approval of the engagement. But after that visit the colonel wrote his daughter a long, loving letter, hinting that he might offer the lovers help.

Eventually the colonel arranged another home for the Greele children. Abba was free. And Bronson had a job offer—from Dr. Charles Windship, the widower of Abba's oldest sister. Another infant school was being started by a society of Owenites, followers of a British mill owner who was a champion of early childhood education. Bronson could be headmaster at a handsome salary.

Bronson said no. He would have had to teach the society's doctrines, and there was much in them he did not approve. He was once again standing by his principles at considerable sacrifice—this time, not just of himself, but of Abba, too.

On January 25, 1830, he made his mind up equally abruptly. He was thirty, Abba was twenty-nine. If they waited any longer for financial security, they might never marry at all.

On Sunday afternoon, the twenty-second of May 1830, Abba and Bronson "stood up" in King's Chapel on Tremont Street and became man and wife. Abba wore a plaid silk walking dress and a fashionable black beaver hat. Their wedding journey was a walk of a few blocks to their new home— one room at Mrs. Newell's boardinghouse at 12 Franklin Street.

FOUR

"... A Crass Crying Brown Baby"

FOR BRONSON AND ABBA, the summer of 1830 was one long honeymoon. They were totally wrapped up in each other.

Soon after the wedding they received an anonymous gift of $2,000, probably from Colonel May. Bronson, too, could make a grand gesture. He took his wife to Spindle Hill to meet his mother. While there, he paid in full the debt he had owed his father—$600, plus $100 in interest. He had proved to the Alcoxes that the family dreamer could turn out well.

During that summer Bronson wrote an essay, "Observations on the Principal Methods of Infant Education." It was one of the best things he ever wrote—clear, organized, and original. In it he demanded that education begin with the *child,* not with *subject matter.* Developing a child's imagination was particularly important, and it was the teacher's responsibility to make learning a pleasure.

In that one essay Bronson literally invented child-centered education and the study of child psychology. Up to then, children had been seen only as "empty vessels" to be filled by the teacher with facts and moral teachings.

The essay was published that autumn and was read by a wealthy Quaker, Reuben Haines. He offered to back Bronson Alcott and his friend William Russell, a Scottish educator, in starting a school in Germantown, Pennsylvania. On December 14, 1830, the Alcotts and Russells set off by coach and steamboat for Philadelphia. Abba was six months pregnant, but she endured the four days of jolting travel because she couldn't bear to miss a moment of the new adventure.

Three months later, Anna Bronson Alcott was born. The new father and mother were overjoyed.

They were still living in a boardinghouse, and for weeks Bronson never left his wife and daughter's side. From the day of Anna's birth, Bronson kept an account of her development. It was the first record of its kind ever kept in the country. Bronson was a natural-born psychologist.

Anna, Bronson was pleased to see, was quiet and peaceful and easy to influence. She took after her father, he decided. She was a very good baby, easy to raise.

Reuben Haines found the Alcotts a house in Germantown called The Pines, where they could live rent free. Among its luxuries were a separate dining room and classroom space for the new school. Abba and Bronson bought their first furniture, including a drop-leaf table of which Abba was quite proud. They used up the rest of the anonymous gift money and had to borrow more from Colonel May.

This didn't bother either Abba or Bronson. The school was succeeding, thanks to Reuben Haines. Spring came, and the peach trees bloomed, and baby Anna played in the garden. Bronson thought she was growing like a "perfect tree."

He saw to it that she wore only loose, simple clothes, so that she could run around easily.

Country life seemed like a fairy tale to the Alcotts. But fairy tales often have a darker side. Bronson sometimes got carried away with his scientific experiments. Once he made a horrible face at Anna, and noticed that she looked terrified. He felt bad about it, but then his scientific curiosity got the better of him. He pulled her hair when she pulled his, to see what she would make of the pain. He let her put her hand in the flame of an oil lamp in order to study her reaction. Bronson was not a cruel person, but he could become so obsessed by his ideas that everything else, including compassion, was swept away.

On November 29, 1832, Bronson's thirty-third birthday, Abba presented him with a second daughter. They named her for Abba's much-loved dead sister—*Louisa May*. Louy, as she was called, was quite a change from the docile Anna.

"*I* was a crass crying brown baby," Louisa wrote in a birthday letter to her father twenty-three years later, "bawling at the disagreeable old world where on a dismal November day I found myself, & began my long fight."

Actually, Louisa almost died during her first week of life. Life at Germantown was becoming harder. Reuben Haines had died, and without his support the school faltered. For Abba, the honeymoon days were over. She longed to be alone with her family but she had to take students in as boarders. William Russell, the Alcotts' one close friend, went back to Boston. The Germantown school failed.

Bronson remembered the Philadelphian who had introduced him to Reuben Haines. Roberts Vaux, like Colonel May, was a wealthy man who had retired from money-making to do good works. He agreed to set Bronson up in a two-room school in Philadelphia, with twenty students.

In April 1833, the Alcotts went back to their former boardinghouse on South Third Street. They had to sell all their fine new furniture. There was no more garden. There were no more servants. But Abba managed to be optimistic. She went to Sunday worship at a Quaker meetinghouse. She made new friends, among them Lucretia Mott, the Quaker feminist. The Philadelphia Anti-Slavery Society had just been founded. Bronson had the Loganian Library, where he could do research, and the companionship of many scholars.

Louisa was now nearly five months old, and Bronson was keeping an "infant diary" on her. He found her disturbing. If Anna was like her father, Louisa was like Abba. She had the same olive skin, abundant dark hair, and the May eyes that seemed to change from dark blue to gray to black. She had Abba's forceful temperament. Bronson's aim with his daughters was to mold them in the image of his spiritual self. It didn't work with Louisa. She was an intensely restless, *physical* being—the very qualities Bronson found tormenting.

Power struggles were going on. Anna was very jealous of the new baby. Louisa, as she grew, wanted to dominate her older sister. Neither wanted to share their mother's attentions. Anna, the perfect child, turned into a little monster, and Louisa threw tantrums.

Bronson was having problems also. He was so concerned with shaping the minds of his pupils that he neglected to teach them regular school subjects. Parents became upset and withdrew their children. Rumors about Bronson's teaching methods began to spread, just as they had at Cheshire. On top of all this, Abba was pregnant again.

All the pressures were making Bronson frantic. At the library he could shut out the world and give himself the education he had never had. He studied Plato and the great modern European writers. He studied classical philosophy and the new romantic philosophy. He developed a new philosophy of his own that was a mix of both, and included the sixteenth-century religious poets. When he went back to the boardinghouse, he found life there just too *intense*.

In April 1834, he made a big decision. He needed to be alone. Abba and the girls must move to a boardinghouse in Germantown. He would stay in Philadelphia by himself. This went against everything he believed about family and the proper upbringing of children, but he did it anyway. It was the only way he could be true to his visions, and he wasn't going to let anyone talk him out of it.

In a way, the drastic solution worked. Without Abba near, he began to long for her again. The children weren't the only ones who had resented having to share Abba's full attention. Bronson spent weekends at Germantown, using his charm to try to force Abba's focus back on him. In early May, he persuaded Abba to come alone to Philadelphia for a day together. It was almost as though their courtship days were back.

Three weeks later Abba had a miscarriage and almost died for lack of proper care. The tragedy seemed like a sign from God. As soon as Abba was well enough, the little family fled back to Boston. While Abba recuperated at her father's house, Bronson rushed about looking for patrons to set him up again in a school.

This time the influential backer he found was a woman. Miss Elizabeth Peabody was *somebody* in Boston. She was one of the famous Peabody sisters of Salem, descendants of one of the old Puritan families. Stout, rumpled, always in a hurry, she was the scholar daughter of a scholar mother who had taught her more than most men learned at universities.

Elizabeth could read ten languages, including Hebrew and Chinese. She ran a school in Brookline, she gave lectures, she cared greatly about children's education, and she had been thinking about starting an experimental school herself. When Bronson showed her the journals kept by his students in Philadelphia, and described his teaching methods, Elizabeth Peabody decided Bronson Alcott was "like an embodiment of intellectual light." It was *he* who should head the school, and *she* would help him. All his life, Bronson had a gift for inspiring women to make sacrifices for his work.

Elizabeth Peabody was part of a new philosophical movement called transcendentalism that was setting Boston intellectuals afire. Transcendentalism was a search for a higher Reality that transcended (rose above) what people were aware of in the bustle of daily life. Transcendentalists tried to find the "nature of Reality" by investigating how their own minds worked, by intuition, and by studying nature and the great philosophers.

One philosopher they thought highly of was Socrates. The Socratic method of teaching, which is still used, was based on the teacher asking a series of leading questions. The student was nudged into coming up with the right conclusion. This was exactly the same kind of method Bronson had been using!

Within hours of meeting Bronson, Elizabeth Peabody found him his first pupil. Soon she found him several more. Bronson located a home for the new school. The Masonic temple on Tremont Street, opposite the Commons, was an elegant new Gothic building, often used for cultural activities. It was the perfect place.

Getting the school ready took a few months. During this time Bronson turned his attention to his little family, which he had moved into a boardinghouse at 21 Federal Street.

He wasn't happy with what he saw. Anna was three by now, and Louisa going on two. They were, quite bluntly, brats. There was none of the sweet harmony Bronson had expected. Anna was becoming rigid and fearful, and Louisa defied all control. Bronson blamed Abba. He complained that he had to do all the disciplining, that she was emotional and inconsistent—two things he hated. What truly puzzled him was that the girls told him point blank that they loved their mother best!

One Monday in October of 1834, five weeks after the new school opened, Bronson seized control at home. He established an orderly routine, and outlawed Abba's occasional spankings. He would lead his daughters, through Socratic questioning, into *choosing* to do what was right.

Bronson's parenting methods were revolutionary. He made bathtime a game, letting the children splash and play and filling the water with handfuls of sweet-smelling herbs. He had great patience in helping Anna overcome her many fears. He invented "quiet time" before bed, talking to his daughters softly as he undressed them and tucked them in. He had them make up stories while they were bathing, and he wove their own experiences into magical bedtime tales.

He taught them the great Judeo-Christian values: love of God, goodness, family; kindness; self-sacrifice; giving to those in need; purity in thought, word, and deed. What was new was that he didn't threaten hellfire and damnation or physical punishment if they disobeyed. No, the guilt bad children suffered was the guilt of having disappointed Papa and Mama. The punishment was the withdrawal of a parent's trust and love.

It seemed logical to Bronson that what children would want most would be to please their parents. *He* had wanted to please the mother who had believed in him against all odds. So he taught his daughters that if a child *really* loved her parents, she would *want* to submit her will to theirs. If she didn't, she would make them terribly disappointed and unhappy.

It is painful to live with that kind of pressure. Bronson believed that he was applying it for his girls' own good. He was sure this was a much more loving way of teaching than the use of physical punishment. Bronson was convinced it was a parent's duty to break a child's will—but gently!—in order to shape the child into a "perfect tree."

Anna, the impressionable, submitted. Louisa never did.

FIVE

"I Will Kindle a Fire
for the Mind"

THE TEMPLE SCHOOL was a huge success.

Abba, remembering past complaints, had been worried about who would teach the children "book learning" like math and Latin. Elizabeth Peabody solved this problem quickly. *She* would be Bronson's assistant. According to her, both Abba and Bronson were "in *rapture*" at her offer.

The two rooms on the top floor of the Masonic temple were a wonder to those first eighteen boys and girls. Bronson had borrowed money to have chairs and desks specially made. Each desk had its own storage shelves and built-in blackboard. On the walls hung fine pictures, and in each corner was a bust of a great man—the philosophers Socrates and Plato, the authors William Shakespeare and Sir Walter Scott. On a bookcase behind Bronson's enormous desk was a large bust of Jesus. There were many books, and plants, and even a green velvet sofa loaned by Elizabeth Peabody.

One of Bronson's rare qualities was his great respect for children, however young. He welcomed his new students with politeness and seated them in a circle. First he asked the children why they came to school, and led them to agree it was to learn "to behave well." Then they talked about what good behavior was, and how to make sure it was always used. Elizabeth Peabody kept a record of it all.

There had never been a school like this before. Bronson encouraged original thought. He didn't mind if a child disagreed with him, so long as it was done politely and with logic. He passed on his love of books, and of putting words on paper. He taught reading and writing in ways not in common use for another hundred years. In his own way, however, he was very strict. He was doing the same thing he had with Anna and Louisa in the nursery—controlling children by persuading them into submission. They gave in because they saw his way was best—or because they were afraid of losing his affection.

Rejection by Bronson Alcott hurt a child worse than the single slap of a ruler on the hand that teacher Bronson would give in private in drastic cases. Worst of all was the threat of being sent to the cloakroom or expelled.

By winter enrollment had doubled, and classes were even held on Saturdays. Elizabeth Peabody couldn't tear herself away, even when there wasn't enough money to pay her small salary. She stayed long hours, and she wrote feverishly, recording everything that happened. The winter temperature fell to below zero, Boston Harbor froze over, and students and teachers gathered close in the icy classroom and warmed themselves with Bronson's eloquence.

"I will kindle a fire for the mind," Bronson told Elizabeth Peabody.

He was creating his own small world there in the Temple School. He was almost beginning to compare himself with the great Hebrew prophets—or to Jesus. He spoke of his students as disciples. Elizabeth Peabody moved into the Bedford Street boardinghouse with the Alcotts, and she and Bronson talked about "high things" far into the night. She had become a part of the Alcott family.

They moved to another boardinghouse on Somerset Court in June 1835, and very soon after that Abba's third child was born. It was another little girl. Bronson named her Elizabeth Peabody Alcott. He had been present at her birth, something almost unheard of at that time.

Lizzie had deep blue eyes and a kind of inner radiance and trust. The journal Bronson kept on her tells not of her physical development but of her spiritual growth. From the first she was her father's "soul mate."

She was a very good baby, and big sister Anna was now a good girl, too. Louisa had a hard time being good. One day, in a fit of jealousy about Lizzie, Louisa shouted out, "I wish she was dead, I will throw her out of the window."

Abba promptly sent Louisa to her room to think things over. Bronson came home to find the child sobbing, convinced no one could love her, not even God. Bronson assured Louisa that she was indeed loved, though she had made everyone, including God, feel very sad. Louisa rushed around giving kisses and apologies to everyone, including Baby.

That summer Elizabeth Peabody's account of Temple School was published under the title *Record of a School*. Elizabeth Peabody was a very lively writer, and the book attracted much attention. She made Bronson's complicated philosophy of educational reform clear and understandable.

The second year of Temple School began with forty pupils. New teachers were added, and important people came to watch the classes. Word of Bronson Alcott's genius was spreading throughout the country.

On Saturday, November 28, the day before Bronson and Louisa's shared birthday, a great festival was held at the Temple School. Three-year-old Louisa was beside herself with excitement. The students crowned Bronson and Louisa with laurel wreaths, and Bronson told students, teachers, and distinguished guests the story of his life. He ended by listing three important things that had happened recently. The first was his becoming a vegetarian and giving up "animal food." Another was his meeting abolitionist publisher William Lloyd Garrison. The third, which had happened three days earlier, was his meeting writer and philosopher Ralph Waldo Emerson.

That festival was probably the greatest moment in the history of the Temple School, but what interested little Louisa May the most was the refreshments that were to follow. At last the program was over. Bronson lifted the birthday girl up on the table and allowed her to give out the cakes. Louisa felt quite important—but the supply of cakes was dwindling rapidly. Eventually there was only one cake left. Two girls were waiting for it. One of them was Louisa. She took no chances; she grabbed the cake.

At once Abba was there, reminding that it was always better to give than to receive. Louisa struggled with her conscience. Finally she did the generous thing. But, as she told family friend Ednah Dow Littlehale Cheney many years later, she never forgot how much she had wanted that "dear plummy cake."

Louisa had many happy memories of the Temple School years to store away: rolling her hoop in Boston Common; the excitement of coasting down the Long Slope, and election days when the Common turned into one great outdoor fair; falling into the Frog Pond and being pulled out by a young black boy. Louisa was becoming quite a tomboy.

The Alcotts didn't live in a boardinghouse anymore. Bronson had rented what he called a mansion, a big wooden house at 26 Front Street, south of the Commons. There was a big yard for the children to play in, and a garden, and Bronson had his study on the second floor. Abba had "hired girls" to help her with the work, for some of the Temple School students boarded with the Alcotts. So did Elizabeth Peabody, and many friends and relatives came to visit.

Bronson bought more and more books. Abba had new furniture and an elegant dinner service of white china. The Sewalls contributed a silver tea-and-coffee service that reflected the gleam of the polished brass on the Franklin stove. But sometimes there were quarrels at the dinner table, particularly about the vegetarian gospel Bronson was now preaching. And after a while Elizabeth Peabody no longer hero-worshiped Bronson Alcott.

Bronson was getting carried away by his new ideas. He always did; it always got him into trouble, and he never noticed until it was too late. Elizabeth Peabody did notice, and she tried to warn him.

"It seems no part of his plan to search the thoughts and views of other minds. . . . He only seems to look in books for what agrees with his own thoughts," she declared with exasperation. She accused him of thinking himself superior to everyone else. Abba became fierce and furious in Bronson's defense, and Elizabeth Peabody cried all night.

What burned in Bronson just then was a determination to

teach his ideas about Jesus to his students. Bronson saw himself and Jesus as being much alike. They had both been born poor and obscure, they had both had lonely childhoods, they had both struggled against society and had been called to preach.

Bronson was so drawn to Jesus the Man that he rejected the Christian doctrine of Jesus' divinity. Unlike most proper Bostonians, Bronson hadn't gone to church in years. While Abba and the girls went to Kings Chapel on Sunday mornings, Bronson stayed home. He had his own church, he said—the Temple School, where he was the preacher.

He began having what he called "Conversations on the Gospels" with his students. He started with the birth of John the Baptist, and went from that to the birth of Jesus. Where had Jesus come from? Where did *any* babies come from? The children struggled with that question but couldn't find the answer. Bronson gave it to them.

He was not teaching anything immoral. He had great respect for marriage and for purity. What he was saying was that physical love between a man and a woman, at its best, could be profoundly spiritual and could lead to a better understanding of God.

This wasn't an original idea; Bronson had read it in the Scriptures. And Bronson's own language, when he explained this to the children, was so poetic that they couldn't understand what he was saying.

But they went home and told their parents what they'd heard. They *did* understand what Bronson was saying, and they were alarmed. There were many reasons for this. One was that the children were so young. Another was that parents wanted any such teaching done by themselves. Many parents believed that innocence was a child's best defense against sin and evil.

Bronson's *Conversations on the Gospels* caused an uproar. Elizabeth Peabody was away at the time, or things might not have gotten so out of hand. While she was gone her youngest sister, Sophia, acted as recorder of Bronson's classes.

Elizabeth Peabody came back in July 1836 and was appalled at what had been going on. She'd been away from the spell of Alcott magic for three weeks, and now saw everything much more clearly. A whispering campaign had started about Bronson, and the Temple School was in danger. Bronson's success with the school had taken place because Elizabeth Peabody had championed his efforts. Now Boston held her responsible. Bronson had humiliated and disgraced her, and he couldn't even see that he had done so.

In August, Elizabeth Peabody resigned. Bronson replaced her with another woman whom he had met through Mr. Emerson.

Like Elizabeth Peabody, Margaret Fuller was a scholar. Like Elizabeth, she fell at least halfway in love with Bronson, although at times she actually disliked him. Margaret was young, even more brilliant than Elizabeth, and far more beautiful. She had, like Bronson, an inner passion and the power to bemuse people's minds. She became Louisa's teacher and her lifelong inspiration.

Once Elizabeth Peabody was away from the Alcotts she began to worry about the written records she and Sophia had kept. She knew Bronson wanted to publish them, just as he had published *Record of a School*. This time he intended to include the children's real names. Boston, Elizabeth Peabody knew, would be roused to fury.

She wrote Bronson a long and deliberately calm letter, advising him not to publish. If he *did* insist on going on, he shouldn't include the children's names, and he shouldn't mention her. Bronson simply ignored her pleas.

On December 22, 1836, Bronson published, at his own expense, the first volume of *Conversations with Children on the Gospels*. More than a hundred copies were sold by Christmas day. A few weeks later the firestorm broke.

Prominent newspapers attacked Bronson for heresy. He was called "either insane or half-witted" and an "ignorant charlatan." His book was called "filthy and godless."

Emerson and others, including Margaret Fuller, wrote letters in defense of Bronson, but they only made things worse. This time Bronson had truly gone too far.

The second volume of *Conversations* came out in February 1837. Only a few copies were sold. Parents withdrew their children from the Temple School. Bronson could no longer pay Margaret Fuller's salary, and she, too, left. Preachers denounced Bronson from their pulpits. Children booed him in the streets. Soon Bronson had no students at all.

Then the creditors attacked. Bronson, it turned out, had borrowed all over the city, from banks and from friends. Up till now, the moneylenders had not worried, trusting in Bronson's Temple School success and his father-in-law's good name. But now the day of reckoning had come.

Where all the money had gone, no one was quite sure. He owed nearly $6,000—an enormous sum, more than most schoolmasters could hope to save in their whole lives. The contents of the school were sold at auction, everything but the bust of Socrates, but the sale only brought a few hundred dollars.

Elizabeth Peabody tried to start a school of her own and found no one would help her. She couldn't even get work. Bronson Alcott's disgrace had rubbed off on her. She and her sister Sophia went back to Salem.

For a while Bronson kept the ghost of a school going in a windowless basement room at the Masonic temple. The

Front Street mansion was given up. The Alcotts moved into a tiny house on Cottage Place, in the South End of Boston. In all the despair, Abba could find one ray of sunlight: She, the girls, and Bronson were alone at last.

Two months later, Abba went into labor prematurely and delivered a dead child. For years Abba's moods had been alternating between high optimism and deep depression. Through it all, she had defended Bronson almost savagely. She had even broken off relations with her father. When Bronson had asked to borrow money to help open the Temple School, Colonel May had obliged. But he had written Abba a brutally frank letter, pointing out all the things she didn't want to face about her husband.

Abba had dashed off a long answer, pointing out that she and Bronson never spent money on themselves. "My husband . . . is just and conscious, honorable and upright," she insisted. Colonel May's bad opinion, she implied, came from the poisonous influence of his second wife. Now, in the wake of the *Conversations* scandal, Abba couldn't even turn to her family for comfort.

What saved her from breakdown was her absolute faith in Bronson, and her dramatic instinct. She would be strong; they would survive. In her need to blame someone, she lashed out at the very people who had tried to give Bronson good advice.

Her main target was Elizabeth Peabody. Elizabeth had dared to criticize the *Conversations* when Bronson was writing them. It was too late to change Lizzie's first name, but Abba could and did change her daughter's middle name from Peabody to Sewall.

What was remarkable in all this storm of public and personal name-calling was Bronson's own behavior. His greatest dreams, and his family's security, had been destroyed. Yet he blamed no one. He answered all the attacks with dignified silence. He mourned the lost books and the lost school, but in private. No one saw him acting other than with gentle dignity. He spent his time writing, studying, and caring for the children. Lizzie, especially, was his comfort. He called her "Psyche" and his "soul mate."

Emerson sensibly urged his friend to give up teaching and concentrate on writing: "[L]eave the impractical world to wag its own way, & sit apart & write your oracles. . . . Write, let them hear or let them forbear—the written word abides." Bronson decided to turn his observations of Lizzie into a book—*Psyche: The Breath of Childhood.*

He had to stop writing temporarily when Abba, for the third time, delivered a premature, stillborn child. For several weeks she herself lingered between life and death. Emerson and others gave money; parents from the Temple School days brought food. Bronson did all the nursing, childcare, and household work. By spring Abba was her old self and Bronson was revising *Psyche,* trying to make it perfect. His changes took any life and clarity out of his writing.

Emerson read the manuscript and tried to be kind. But Bronson knew Emerson was right. "My might is not in my pen," he admitted in despair. He knew he had a "calling," but what was it? Neither being philosopher-peddler nor philosopher-teacher had been successful.

One night Bronson had a vivid dream. He saw himself as a peddler-*talker.* Soon after that he began giving informal lectures, which he called "conversations," in people's homes. He rarely made as much as a dollar in pay, sometimes a lot less, but he became convinced he had discovered his life's work. It was, he announced, a "Ministry of Talking."

SIX

"This Is the Winter of My Discontent"

BY LOUISA'S SIXTH BIRTHDAY the Alcotts had moved again. Now they shared half a house with the Russell family at 6 Beech Street. Once more Abba had no home of her own. Bronson no longer had a real school but taught a few very young children at home. There was very little money coming in.

In January 1839 Abba's despised stepmother died. The shock filled Abba with remorse. She wrote to her father, seeking a reconciliation. Colonel May, old, deaf, and grieving, was glad to be reunited with his favorite daughter. Once again Louisa had the run of the Federal Court house and its wonderful library. Grandfather May, in his old-fashioned knee breeches with their sparkling buckles, took Louisa on his lap and told her stories. Abba and her father sang hymns together, just as they used to do when she was young.

Bronson, too, was remembering his childhood. He wrote his mother a long letter, thanking her for all she had done for him and for one particular trait that she had passed on.

"I am full of hope," he wrote, "and everything looks encouraging. As to money, that you know, is one of the last of my anxieties. I have many friends, and am making more daily, and have only to be true to my principles, to get not only a useful name, but bread and shelter, and raiment."

That statement explains Bronson and his lifelong financial troubles. He always believed that so long as he did what he was sure was right, *somebody else* would provide for his family's needs. "I am still the same Hoper that I have always been," he told his mother. He closed the letter with the news that Abba was expecting another baby in the spring. He was sure that this time it would be a boy.

The baby was born on Saturday, April 6, 1839, and it *was* a boy. But it lived only a few minutes. Abba was nearly forty now, and had lost several children before they had even lived. She was desperate to find a reason, but she never did. And she never forgot.

Bronson had to take his son's tiny body to be laid away in the May family vault. Old Colonel May sent round a note, asking if he could go with Bronson. Together the two sorrowing men, so often at odds, went through the April Sunday morning to the Old Granary Burial Ground, where so many patriots were buried, on Tremont Street. Afterward Bronson went straight to his journal. The dank atmosphere of the vault had filled him with doubt and horror.

"Let me tread the sweet plots of Hope and breathe the incense of her flowering glories. *There is no past in all her borders,*" Bronson wrote. He drew a line under the last sentence to emphasize it.

He was still conducting a school of sorts at home. Two

months after his son was born and died, he admitted his last pupil. Her name was Susan Robinson, and she was black.

Bronson knew perfectly well that in running up the flag of his own beliefs, he was ringing down the curtain on his teaching career. Boston was for abolition—slavery had already been outlawed in all northern states—but not for integration. All the parents except the Robinsons and the Russells promptly took their children out of school.

Bronson had forced Boston to face its own hypocrisy and prejudice. He had also destroyed all hope of a future there. It had been a foolhardy—and very courageous—thing to do.

Eight-year-old Anna Alcott wrote about Susan Robinson in her journal entries of January 5, 18, and 21, 1840. That is the only record of the incident that exists. The Robinsons were probably members of the free black community in Boston and possibly among the Alcotts' abolitionist friends.

Ralph Waldo Emerson, Bronson's greatest friend, was by now living eighteen miles west of Boston in Concord, Massachusetts. The pretty town was famous as the place where the Redcoats had first fired on the Massachusetts farmers and set off the War for Independence. Emerson himself had grown up there in the Old Manse, his grandparents' home. Now he hoped to make Concord an intellectual center and the home of transcendentalism.

"Come to Concord," Emerson wrote the Alcotts. Bronson loved the idea. He would be a farmer-philosopher. "My garden shall be my poem," he wrote.

But before the Alcotts could move to Concord, they needed a house and money. The Mays provided enough funds for the move itself. Bronson decided to simply leave his

Boston debts behind and hope that his creditors wouldn't find him.

Friends found the house—a tenant cottage on land owned by the Hosmer family. It was small and sprawling, one of New England's add-on houses that had started with one room and then had others added. It was dove-brown in color, and Bronson promptly named it Dove Cottage.

With the house came barns, sheds, and one and three-quarter acres of land. Dove Cottage was half a mile from the center of town but very near the Emersons' square white house. The Alcotts planned to raise their own food, and Bronson meant to "hire out" as a farmhand.

They moved in on a wintery April Fool's Day, 1840. All the branches of the skeleton trees were sheathed with ice that chimed and twinkled and glittered in the wind. To nine-year-old Anna, seven-year-old Louisa, and Lizzie, who was almost five, it was an enchanted world.

Abba was ecstatic. She sang and worked all day long. She was in a hurry to make their new home livable. Bronson also worked around the clock—hard, physical labor. He repaired sagging doorsteps, he trimmed bushes and planted trees and hung trellises. Fences and outbuildings turned white as if by magic. By the first of May, the fields were plowed and spring planting had begun. And the girls, for the first time, were enrolled in a school outside their home. Anna studied from the Thoreau brothers, John and Henry, at Concord Academy. Louisa and Lizzie attended classes taught by Mary Russell at the Emerson home.

The Alcott girls found Concord life different and exciting. The Hosmer children lived right next door. Henry Joseph became Anna's object of adoration. Lydia and Lizzie played dolls together. Louisa and Cyrus Hosmer rampaged joyously through the woods, climbing trees, daring each other to dangerous feats such as jumping from the barn's highest beam.

The barn was a perfect place to put on plays. Louisa, in Grandfather May's old military uniform, played heroes to her heart's content. And there was all of Concord—town, woods, and river—to explore.

Louisa made grown-up friends also. Emerson was her first great crush. Henry Thoreau, who was like a boy himself and used all Concord as a classroom, taught the children about nature.

Breakfast at Dove Cottage was porridge and water and unleavened bread. Afterward the girls studied with Bronson for an hour. They would read from the Bible, and Bronson would teach spelling by twisting his long body into the shapes of all the letters. After that he would read a story, or talk to them about the new kind of life he was trying to shape for them, and why they shouldn't eat meat or drink milk anymore. Dinner, at midday, was potatoes or boiled rice, vegetables, and more unleavened bread.

Lizzie's fifth birthday came in June. The Alcotts always made birthdays into magical, day-long celebrations, with garlands of leaves and flowers and special poems and letters they wrote each other. Soon afterward came the Fourth of July, with a twenty-six-gun salute at sunrise. Crowds poured into the center of town to hear the Townsend Light Infantry military band and watch the grand parade.

Toward the end of July, Louisa was sent on a six-week visit with Grandfather May. When she returned home, she found an intruder in Dove Cottage. A new baby sister had been born at dawn on the twenty-sixth of July. Louisa wanted nothing to do with her.

The new baby was a real Alcott, with golden hair and blue eyes like her father. What she didn't have for several months was a name. Eventually she was given her mother's name—Abba May. The family called her Abby or Ab; as she grew up, she decided to be known as May.

The Alcotts' last child, and the only one not to receive intense attention from her parents, May was brought up mostly by her sisters. Anna mothered the new baby, and Lizzie played with her. Louisa took over the kitchen, where she could relieve her moods by banging pots and pans. She was going on eight years old at the time.

By now Bronson Alcott knew he would never have a son. He wrote about how beautiful May was, but he didn't try to mold her or control her. He was all wrapped up in the birth of a new transcendentalist magazine, *The Dial*.

Bronson looked forward to writing for *The Dial*. He used his journal as practice and changed his writing style completely. Instead of rambling, he tried to write like Emerson and to "compress" his thoughts as Emerson had advised him. He called these writings "Orphic Sayings," a term derived from the character Orpheus in Greek mythology.

When Emerson read them, he was at a loss for words. *Dial* editor Margaret Fuller and the other transcendentalists didn't think much of the Orphic Sayings either. Because of their respect for Bronson Alcott, they published them anyway. It was a bad decision. Bronson was trying to come to grips with profound questions about the universe, but he did so in ways that were open to misunderstanding. *The Dial* and its writers, especially Bronson, were laughed at everywhere.

All the other writers eventually won great respect. Bronson lost what little public respect he had left. Once he had been considered a dangerous lunatic. Now he was regarded as just a boring old fool. He was forty years old, and he was a success at nothing.

Even Abba's belief in him was becoming tarnished. "Mr.

Alcott can earn nothing here but food," Abba wrote in desperation to her brother Sam as the summer of 1840 dragged to a close. "Fuel must be *paid for,* water must be *paid* for, the land out of which we would dig our bread must be *paid* for—what is to be done?" Bronson still believed life without money should be possible, but his wife had learned a harsh lesson. *Someone* in the family had to earn money. It was either that, or starve.

Abba begged her father to help, but the colonel had had enough. She begged Sam to find Bronson a job, but Sam had troubles of his own. He had lost his pulpit because of his abolitionist activities. He offered to take the Alcotts in but had no other help to give. Bronson could always get a teaching job if he'd just teach the way he was supposed to. That, Sam pointed out to Abba, Bronson would never do.

Abba still flew fiercely to Bronson's defense, but by now she knew that he brought most of his problems on himself. Abba had to share some of the blame. She admired her husband's dedication to his principles—but she also wanted the kind of life she had had as a May of Boston.

Louisa's eighth birthday came and went. 1841 began as a terrible year. Abba was slowly realizing that if the family was to survive, she herself would have to earn the money. Many women she knew had careers. Elizabeth Peabody was supporting her parents with income from her little bookstore. Margaret Fuller, as editor, lecturer, and journalist, supported her family, too. Abba decided to take in sewing. Anna and Louisa could help. Already they both knew how to sew fine seams. "My girls shall have trades," Abba vowed. She didn't want them to end up dependent on the money of their future husbands.

Down the road in his fine home, Emerson, too, was worrying about the Alcotts. He had brought them to Concord, and he wanted them to stay there. He suggested the Alcotts move in with his family. The two wives would share the housekeeping, and Bronson could help with work on the land.

Sharing a life with Ralph Waldo Emerson, the one man who really appreciated him, came close to being Bronson's idea of heaven. Abba's idea of heaven was a home of her own. She didn't want to share space, housekeeping, or her husband. She persuaded Bronson to turn down Emerson's invitation.

In February news came from Boston that old Colonel May was dying. Abba hurried to his bedside to join Sam in keeping deathwatch.

Losing her adored father was a blow to Abba, and his will was another. The colonel had divided his wealth evenly between his three living children and the descendants of his nine children who had died. Abba, the most in need, therefore received only her mother's silver teapot and a few thousand dollars. Even that money was put in trust, not in her own control. The colonel had made sure Bronson couldn't get his hands on it.

For Abba, this shock was almost greater than she could bear. She was deeply hurt and furiously angry.

"This is the winter of my discontent," Bronson wrote in his journal, paraphrasing *Richard III*. He should, like Shakespeare, have written "*our* discontent."

Spring came to Concord, and then summer; then autumn and Louisa's ninth birthday. Parents then, as now, tried to shield their children from finding out about marriage and money troubles. But Anna was already a too-proper and dutiful "little old lady" of ten, and Louisa had shot up into a tall, thin tomboy who noticed far too much. They had to know when their parents stopped sharing a bed for a while and

Bronson slept instead in Lizzie's room. They had to understand what it meant when they outgrew their clothes and had no way to replace them. They had to realize, when the evening meals became just bread and water, that it wasn't *only* because of Bronson's queer ideas.

"Queer" was becoming one of Louisa's favorite words. She used it to mean interesting, original, or fun. But life at Dove Cottage was growing queer in a totally different, and far more frightening, sense.

Aunt Hannah Robie came for a Thanksgiving visit, bringing a bundle of badly needed hand-me-down clothes. Supper that first night was bread and water. Thanksgiving dinner the next day was squash, potatoes, and apple pandowdy. Afterward Abba asked Aunt Robie to sell the precious silver teapot that had been Grandmother May's. Bronson sat wrapped in silence except for when he criticized Abba for serving tea. Drinking anything but water now went against Bronson's principles.

All at once he broke in on the women's talk with a burst of black despair. He couldn't live any longer with such loads of debt! They would have to live even more simply! He would take on the work of chopping fuel for their neighbors!

Aunt Robie made a sarcastic comment, and went back to Boston sick at heart. The story of the Alcotts' destitution began to leak all over Boston. Abba's moods grew black, and she began making biting comments about transcendentalism. She was close to terror, and Bronson was close to breakdown, physical or mental.

Louisa noticed it all, and she remembered. Someday she would write about it, but for now she just stored it away behind her big, dark, all-seeing blue-gray eyes.

SEVEN

"The Newness"

CHANGES WERE ABOUT TO OCCUR that would shake Louisa's world. For four years now, while Bronson Alcott's reputation had diminished in the New World, it had been growing in the Old.

Back in the Temple School days, Elizabeth Peabody had introduced a visiting English journalist to Bronson. Harriet Martineau was a feminist and abolitionist and even more radical than the transcendental reformers. She had angered Abba by criticizing Bronson. But she had taken a copy of *Record of a School* back to England, where she showed it to a bankrupt businessman named James Pierrepont Greaves. Greaves was a mystic and an educational reformer and had spent years studying from the great Swiss educator Johann Pestalozzi, whom Sam May and Bronson Alcott both admired. He reacted to *Record of a School* exactly the way Sam

May had reacted to that paper on Bronson Alcott's Cheshire School experiment years before. He became an Alcott admirer and began inviting Bronson to come to England.

Letters between Bronson Alcott and his English "fan club" began crossing the Atlantic as fast as ships could carry them. James Greaves had the same kind of strong, magnetic personality that Bronson had. He, too, had a gift for talking, a dream of creating a perfect world, and an inner excitement that was contagious. He believed in a "Love Spirit" that gave life meaning, and a "Sacred Socialism" as a way of life. He and his followers thought Bronson Alcott was a living embodiment of the "Love Spirit."

There were great differences between the American transcendentalists and the English reformers, but neither seemed to realize that in their excitement. The Greaves group founded an experimental school outside of London, and they named it Alcott House. By 1842, Alcott House was a big success. Bronson longed to see it. As the Alcotts' poverty grew harsher, and Abba's tongue grew sharper, that longing turned into an obsession.

As Bronson Alcott's star had fallen, Ralph Waldo Emerson's had risen. Mr. Emerson, too, was a philosopher and talker, but a practical one. His lecture tours made him rich. Life at his house was as comfortable and orderly as life at Dove Cottage was frantic and frustrated. A wall was going up between the two men who had once been like brothers. Bronson was jealous of Waldo; Waldo was impatient with Bronson's intense self-absorption.

In January 1842, a form of scarlet fever struck the Emerson house, and within days the Emersons' five-year-old son was dead. In his sorrow, Emerson remembered the sad condition of his old friend's life. All Emerson's money had not been able to save his son, but it might save Bronson. Emerson provided the funds for a six-month visit to England and Alcott House.

It took three months for all the arrangements to be made. On May 8, 1842, Bronson Alcott boarded the *Rosalind* for the journey. He took with him two trunks of transcendentalist papers, a few clothes, ten English sovereigns (gold coins worth one English pound each), and credit for twenty pounds more. He also took several loaves of unleavened bread, crackers, a basket of apples, and a jar of applesauce—transcendentalist food for the journey. Behind him he left a load of debts, fields to be plowed and planted, and a wife and children for whom he suddenly felt a wave of overwhelming love.

Life was much more serene at Dove Cottage with the head of the house away. Abba was miserable with loneliness for him at first. But Bronson's youngest brother, twenty-four-year-old Junius, came to stay and help with the farming. Abba was busy with her seamstress work and fending off bill collectors. She poured out her soul in letters to brother Sam, and the May family came through with money to pay off some of the debts.

Letters came from Bronson constantly. They were full of his love for Abba and the girls, and of the wonderful ideas that were coming to him in England. Mr. Greaves had died, but Bronson had found two new soul mates, Alcott House headmaster Henry Gardner Wright and a mysterious man named Charles Lane.

The letters talked about something Bronson called "the Newness." He was very vague about exactly what that meant. But he was certain that the time had come for a New Eden, and that the place for it was not in the Old World, but in New England.

In the meanwhile, exciting things were happening in Concord. On June 24, Abba and the girls staged a birthday party for Lizzie in a barn draped with sheets and elegant with candlelight. Lizzie was seven now, gentle and quiet. The Fourth of July was celebrated. Henry Thoreau was living at the Emerson house and was like a Pied Piper to all the village children. May's second birthday was celebrated with a picnic down the river, with Uncle Junius doing the rowing. And in the Old Manse near the bridge, where Emerson had grown up, were newlyweds—Elizabeth Peabody's youngest sister, Sophia, and her bridegroom, the romantically haunted-looking writer Nathaniel Hawthorne.

By autumn, Dove Cottage was electric with anticipation. Bronson was coming home, bringing new friends. They arrived in Boston harbor on the *Leland* in the early morning of Friday, October 21, 1842. By afternoon they were on the stagecoach for Concord.

The reunion was straight out of a storybook. Dove Cottage was "newly swept and garnished for the reception of my husband and his friends." Abba stood in the doorway with her daughters clustered around her to welcome the wanderer and his English friends. Henry Wright, in fur cap and collar, was still haggard from seasickness. Charles Lane was gaunt-faced, with strange expressionless eyes. His son William was about Louisa's age. Bronson looked thin and worn (he had been seasick the whole three weeks, and hadn't eaten at all the last seven days), but his eyes were alight with excitement and love. The winter of his discontent was past.

"Mother, what makes me so happy?" Louisa burst out when they were alone. Abba, her own voice husky, answered, "Kind friends. Dear Husband."

The visitors were crowded into Dove Cottage for the night, and the next day Emerson invited the Englishmen to stay with him while they were in America. After a week they were back at Dove Cottage. Lane didn't approve of the luxury in which the Emersons lived, nor the food they ate.

Day by day, life at Dove Cottage changed.

Charles Lane took over Bronson's study, where a cheerful wood fire burned. He slept there at night and worked there all through the day. The upstairs bedrooms were unheated. Henry Wright took one. That left one bedroom, and a hall alcove, for the six Alcotts.

The travelers had brought many trunks and packing cases, all filled with books. The dust of those books filled the close air of the cottage just as Charles Lane's talk of "the Newness" did. Louisa soon found out what "the Newness" meant. It was cold sponge baths at dawn, and harsh linen towels. It was breakfast in a circle around the fireplace—no plates (why wash dishes?), just unleavened bread, apples, and potatoes, held in one's lap on a napkin. It was the same food over again at midday dinner, sitting around a table this time.

Charles Lane directed all the conversation. Mostly he and Bronson talked, and the others listened. The two men began going about together, giving speeches and telling people about the New Eden. Henry Wright gave speeches, too, but didn't get as much attention. Unfortunately he himself gave a good deal of attention to a woman named Mary Gove. She had left a husband who mistreated her and so lost custody of her children. Wright himself had a wife and new baby back in England.

Exactly what happened no one knows for sure. There was a scandal. There was also a huge fight between Wright, Lane, and Bronson Alcott. Wright left Concord, then America, and died a few years later.

Louisa was no longer asking "What makes me so happy?" As winter set in, life in Dove Cottage had become very cold and bleak. The huge differences between Bronson's views of a New Eden, and Charles Lane's, were becoming all too apparent. Lane resented the time and attention Bronson "wasted" on his family. He resented anyone else having a chance to talk. The children's lives were full of rigid restrictions. Abba couldn't get a word in edgewise. They all sat silent while Charles Lane ranted about how peculiar maternal instinct was, and how barbarous the whole idea of a family circle.

Charles Lane had been married. He had other children besides William. But he found personal relationships distasteful, especially relationships with women. He saw wife and family as alien things that tempted man from pursuing his inner life, and were therefore evil. Bronson loved his family, and believed that human love, like the love of God, was divine. But Bronson was also torn between the pulls of family and his inner journey. How torn, Louisa wouldn't understand for several years. But she knew something was wrong at Dove Cottage.

On Christmas Eve, everybody knew this. Abba walked out. She took Louisa and young William Lane with her and fled to her relatives in Boston, leaving Bronson and the other girls behind. For the first time, Louisa experienced a May kind of Christmas, warm and noisy, with uncles and aunts and cousins.

Two days later Charles Lane showed up at the May house in Boston and charmed everyone. On January 2, Abba received a New Year's letter from Bronson, begging her to return. A few days later, Abba and Louisa were back in Concord. But the trouble wasn't wiped out, only papered over.

Through the first half of 1843, "the Newness" went on. Charles Lane gave the girls violin lessons. He made a real effort to win Abba over. Abba began going around looking for a place to found the New Eden, as Bronson and Lane were doing. And life grew more regimented and more plain.

Bronson had hoped to woo Emerson into the New Eden, but Emerson was full of scorn. Lane detested Emerson also. But Lane and Bronson were winning other converts. Soon there was a small group of people ready to join the Consociate Family whenever a home for it was found. Lane, who had been shocked to discover how penniless the Alcotts were, was now resigned to personally financing the New Eden.

Eventually two locations were selected. The first, Bronson's favorite, was near the Cliffs, the picnic ground where May's birthday had been celebrated. It was close to Walden Pond, only a few miles from Concord. The other was fourteen miles away, on the edge of forest. There were ninety acres of woodland and a dilapidated farmhouse.

Lane acted quickly, seeing a way at last to pry Bronson free from Emerson's influence. He bought the old farm and paid off Bronson's debts. Abba talked Sam May into helping with the mortgage payments.

On the first of June 1843, a clear and unusually cold day, the pilgrims set out for their New Jerusalem.

EIGHT

The Consociate Family

THE NEW JERUSALEM—a New Eden for a new kind of family—lay on the edge of wilderness and mountains. The nearest neighbor was a mile away. The house Charles Lane had bought, with Sam May as a reluctant sponsor, wasn't even on a road. The little procession, in wagon and on foot, had to roll down the sloping fields to the barn-red, unshuttered farmhouse. But the views of Mount Wachusset and Mount Monadnock were glorious, and the trees, to Louisa's practiced eye, looked great for climbing.

The family was too tired even to explore. They ate their supper of potatoes, bread, and water quickly and fell asleep on blankets on the floor while it was still light.

They were up at dawn to begin settling in. The main room downstairs was called the long kitchen. At back, the old colonial kitchen jutted off to the right. The left side of the

62

house held the dining room and living room, both small and square. From the tiny entry, steep narrow stairs led up to the three bedrooms. Another, even steeper stair wound to a doll-size attic beneath the eaves. This was where the children would sleep.

Everything was almost unlivable. The barns were ramshackle. But the vegetarian Consociate Family didn't intend to keep animals anyway. It was "all arable land, easily cultivated . . . adapted to the culture of grains, herbs, roots, and fruit . . . the 15 acres of oak, maple, walnut, chestnut, some pine . . . quite sufficient for fuel," Bronson wrote. Already there were cherry, peach, and apple trees. Bronson was very fond of apples. In high hopes they named the place Fruit-lands.

There were twelve members of the Consociate Family that June. Five of them—the Alcott girls and William Lane—were younger than thirteen. The first three adults were Bronson and Abba Alcott and Charles Lane. Next to come was twenty-year-old Samuel Larned. He had been part of a group of anarchists and mystics that Bronson had visited in Rhode Island. Before coming to Fruitlands he had been at another Utopian experiment called Brook Farm.

Then came Abram Wood—or Wood Abram, as he rechristened himself. He was a friend of Henry David Thoreau (who had originally been named David Henry). Wood Abram was dark and silent. Like Thoreau, he was most at ease with children. He helped Abba Alcott with childcare and bread-baking.

Abraham Everett was known as "the Plain Man." He was forty-two, a cooper (barrelmaker), and a hard worker. He was rumored to have recently been released from an insane asylum.

Samuel Bower was a Yorkshireman and had been an

Owenite and part of the Alcott House group in England. He called himself a "Sacred Socialist" and believed in nudism.

Another "family member" lived nearby. He was an elderly farmer named Joseph Palmer. Although a Christian, he was called "the Old Jew" because of the bushy white beard that he wore as a protest against shaving. He was an experienced farmer, a shrewd and intelligent man. He lent the Consociate Family tools, equipment, his own labor, and—over the protests of Charles Lane—his cow and bull, to pull a plow.

Within two weeks eleven acres had been planted with barley, rye, oats, and maize for bread and cereal; peas and beans, melons and squash, and potatoes. Turnips and carrots would be planted later. No one seemed to notice it was very late in the year for planting.

The house was swept and scrubbed and ordered. Like every Alcott home, however plain, it took on a stark elegance that had its own beauty. The small dining room became Charles Lane's study also and the children's classroom.

In the hot, serene days of summer, life shaped into a routine much like that in medieval monasteries. Everyone rose at five and took what Louisa in her journal called "cold baths" and said she "loved." Actually they were primitive shower baths, with water poured from a pitcher onto a bather shivering behind a screen of sheets. Sometimes baths were put off until the day's work was over.

Everyone dressed in loose linen tunics and bloomers, an outfit devised by Bronson and Charles Lane. They wore sunbonnets or wide-brimmed linen hats. Shoes were canvas, for leather was forbidden. All this was like a uniform—or a religious habit.

After often-backbreaking morning chores, they gathered for deep talk and a communal meal. As the food became more and more limited, it was consumed with more and more ritual. The first cup of water of the day was celebrated with a song. As at Dove Cottage, the celebrants received their breakfast bread wafer and apple slice in their napkin-covered hands. It was all very much like the Episcopalian communion ritual that had appealed so strongly to the teen-age Bronson.

Dinner was eaten around the table at midday. In the afternoon came time for writing, thinking, reading—or, in Louisa's case, running with the wind down the hills or climbing trees. Trees provided her with a place where she could be alone. After dinner there was singing, reading aloud, even (surprising in descendants of the Puritans) dancing or playing cards. Above all, there was reading and discussion of books.

Bronson and Abba Alcott read everything—Shakespeare, the seventeenth-century poets, Greek and Roman and medieval classics, the Protestant reformers, eastern religious works, current writers like Dickens and Goethe and Maria Edgeworth, even "scandalous" writers like Lord Byron. Their daughters did, too. To these parents, a good book was a good book, regardless of its subject matter and difficult (or controversial) vocabulary.

Lizzie's eighth birthday was celebrated by all the Family members in a bower of flowers. A pine tree in the back woods was hung with presents. Everyone wore wreaths of oak leaves and marched in procession, with songs by all and violin music by Charles Lane.

On July Fourth, Emerson came to visit. All his transcendental circle was now scattered, and he missed Bronson. But he never came to Fruitlands again.

In spite of the hard work and meager food, there was at first much that Louisa could love about life at Fruitlands. Bronson was charged with enthusiasm and hope, like someone swept up in the vortex of a whirlwind. He made the children's lessons fun. Abba sang at her work. As at Dove Cottage, she set up a "private post office" where the Alcotts could leave small gifts and messages for each other. Both Abba and Bronson wrote notes in the children's journals, and soon Louisa's journal became a private conversation between herself and her mother.

Louisa also had children her own age to play with, for the Lovejoys lived only a mile away and the Hosmers a few miles farther. There were dares to be made, trees to be climbed, poems to be written. In the beginning, these made up for the endless ironing, meager food, and Mr. Lane.

By midsummer the Massachusetts heat hung like a cloud over Fruitlands, and even the wind was suffocating. The crops were ripening. Restlessness was stirring in the Family.

Visitors—often perfect strangers—came and went. They stayed for a while or came for a single day. One who stayed, the only woman beside Abba Alcott, was a plump middle-aged spinster named Ann Page. She taught the children music. They hated her. To Louisa's relief, Miss Page left after a stormy fight with Abba.

Bronson Alcott and Charles Lane went off to visit Brook Farm, another communal-living experiment nearby. They considered its craft shops, school and library, and other practical features to be far too much luxury. They also visited other Utopian communities and any people they thought might help Fruitlands. Often these visits took place when they were badly needed in the Fruitlands fields.

Farm work had to be done whether the two men were there or not, and the visitors had to be tended to. Abba, mixing metaphors with abandon, grumbled that Fruitlands was like a public tavern and herself the galley slave. One visitor asked, incredulously, whether there weren't any working animals on

Norma Johnston

FRUITLANDS

the farm. Ignoring the existence of Joseph Palmer's cow and bull, Abba snapped back, "Yes! One woman!"

Lane and the Alcotts expected to win new members into the Consociate Family. Instead people came to gawk, and left to marvel or to laugh. Abraham Everett dropped out and in as the spirit moved him. Samuel Larned left for good. Samuel Bower—in his skin or in a sheet, depending on who was telling the story—frightened the surrounding farmers by haunting the woods in the dark of night.

Charles Lane took over the children's education, and the fun vanished from the lessons. The crops—not as successful as hoped—were maturing. The adults began facing the necessity of moving to another, better farm for the winter. Bronson and Charles Lane increased their visits to other communities and potential backers. Once they "paid" for a ferryboat ride by holding a "conversation" and refused to accept the coins the shocked passengers collected for them. Lane began comparing Abba unfavorably with the Shaker women, who lived together apart from their men. Abba resented being shut out of the men's intellectual talk.

Anna was becoming more than ever the "good child," making bouquets and poems to keep the others happy. Her journal concentrated obsessively on what was "beautiful." Most of the pages in Louisa's Fruitlands journal she herself destroyed years later. But hints are visible in what remains, especially the references to how life was "better" when her father and Mr. Lane weren't there.

There were worms in the apples of the New Eden. One worm was poverty, and another was conflicting desires. Mr. Lane desired a Paradise that had almost nothing of the physical about it—not food, not money, not love, not family ties. Abba desired a harmonious home like that of her childhood, with herself and Bronson as the gracious householders and hosts of their "dear friends." Bronson was torn between those conflicting pulls that came, not just from these two he loved, but from his own divided nature.

Bronson began running frantically, as he often did at such times. To New York, to Rhode Island, to Connecticut, to New Hampshire with Charles Lane. Back and forth to Boston (on foot) in a single day, over and over. After one of those trips, Bronson came down with dysentery so severe that he almost died. He began talking about death repeatedly. Abba, again terrified, wrote to her brother. Sam offered to come himself to Fruitlands, but Abba put him off. If a crisis came she would send for Emerson, who "has good sense enough not to be afraid of human aids for human ends." She was referring to medical treatment and proper food.

The Alcott-Lane "peddling trips" went on. More was at stake than crops or converts, and even the children knew it. The walls between upstairs rooms at Fruitlands were not thick, and Louisa and Anna could hear their parents' nighttime arguments. They could hear when Abba cried.

"I rose at five and had my bath," Louisa wrote in her journal during the first week of September 1843. "I love cold water! Then we had our singing-lesson with Mr. Lane. . . . [I] ran on the hill till nine, and had some thoughts,—it was so beautiful up there. . . . Father asked us what was God's noblest work. Anna said *men,* but I said *babies.* Men are often bad; babies never are. We had a long talk, and I felt better after it, and *cleared up.* . . . I felt sad because I have been cross today, and did not mind Mother. I cried, and then I felt better. . . . I get to sleep saying poetry,—I know a great deal."

"Father and Mr. Lane have gone to N.H. to preach. It was very lovely," Louisa wrote on Sunday, September 24. "I was cross to-day, and I cried when I went to bed. I made good resolutions, and felt better in my heart. If I only *kept* all I make, I should be the best girl in the world. But I don't, and so am very bad."

All through the lean summer the Family's hopes had been pinned on the harvest to come. Now it was autumn. The fields were like a pale gold sea of barley. And Bronson and Charles Lane had gone off down the road on another walking tour, their linen tunics flapping against their linen trousers as they strode away. Abba and the children kept on with the household work, the spinning and the weaving and the sewing. Even little Lizzie already knew how to use her needle. But in Charles Lane's absence, there was a chance to write and dream; for Louisa to run barefoot through the brooks and fields, with her skin getting brown and her dark hair flying free.

Suddenly, one afternoon when Abba was alone at Fruitlands with the children, the wind sprang up, turning the acres of barley stalks into rippling waves. The tall trees shook and shivered like ghostly figures. The sky darkened, though it was still day.

Rain was about to come, in a torrential storm. Already the wind, like a giant's threshing tool, was whipping the heads off the trembling stalks of barley. In the vegetable garden, plants were bent over like bruised reeds. All their summer's hard work, all their food for winter, could be destroyed in the twinkling of an eye. *And Bronson wasn't there.*

Abba shouted for the children over the roaring wind. At her orders, they dragged laundry baskets outdoors, ran to the cupboards for her precious handmade linen sheets. Then, battered by the winds, they worked for hours—gathering, harvesting, dragging sheets full of precious harvest to the barn. They worked till arms and shoulders ached, and backs were near to breaking, trying desperately to salvage the food on which their lives depended.

The dreadful day sealed the end of Fruitlands's hopes. Years later, Louisa would turn the experience into a dark satire that she titled *Transcendental Wild Oats*. Meanwhile, at Fruitlands in October of 1843, a greater storm was building.

When Louisa awoke on the eighth, "the first thought I got was, 'It's Mother's birthday: I must be very good.' . . . I had a moss cross and a piece of poetry for her. . . . I wish I was rich, I was good, and we were all a happy family this day." Four days later: "Mother and Lizzie are going to Boston. I shall be very lonely without dear little Betty, and no one will be as good to me as mother."

Abba spent two days with brother Sam in Lexington. She was fighting for the survival, not of the Consociate Family, but of her own, and she was close to the breaking point.

The tension at Fruitlands came from an issue beyond the lack of food or money, beyond the lack of converts. It went to the heart of the meaning of the word *family*.

Abba was used to defending her husband fiercely against ridicule or scorn. She was used to his moods seesawing from euphoria to despair. She loved him deeply, admired his following his conscience no matter what the cost. Because of that love, she put up with his experiments, put up with poverty, put up with what is now called a macrobiotic diet. But she could not put up with Charles Lane as her rival.

Charles Lane was the latest and most dangerous of the male friends in whom Bronson thought he had found a soul mate. The life that Charles Lane was slowly wooing Bronson into seemed very strange to Westerners of their day or ours. But it was much like that lived by medieval monks or eastern holy men who wandered the earth in perpetual poverty with their begging bowls—pilgrims with no personal or geographic ties. People gave them food and shelter, and considered themselves blessed to do so. The holy men, following their call, gave blessings, prayers, and wisdom with no thought of gain. It was a vision that had a powerful allure to the lonely dreamer from Spindle Hill. But there was no place in that vision for a wife and children.

NINE

"Diaries of a Wilful Child"

WINTER CLOSED IN on Massachusetts that November of 1843. Winds howled down the hill of barren fields and rattled the windows of the old red house. Food was running out, and wood for fuel. Charles Lane thundered his favorite word: "ABSTAIN!"

The Consociate Family was to abstain from—do without—tea and coffee, meat, milk, and warm bath water. They were to abstain from hiring workers, or from being hired; from doing business or owning property; from any organized religion. If Charles Lane had his way, the Family would also abstain from personal relationships and family ties.

Bronson was in torment. For these past long months he had struggled to know himself. Now he was face to face with his own duality and the need to choose: Charles Lane and the monastic life of the mind? Or Abba, daughters, and a real home of his own?

Snow came, and the whole house shivered and starved. Charles Lane forbade cutting more wood or grinding grain. The less the body was coddled, the purer grew the mind, he preached. Sickness swept through Fruitlands like one more bitter wind. Young William Lane lay in bed a whole month, not even able to lift his head. His father nursed him, grumbling, until he, too, fell ill. Louisa had a continual headache and a racking cough that triggered pain in her side and the rheumatism that was to plague her all her life. Only Anna was temporarily safe and warm with Cousin Louisa Willis in Boston.

The crisis was building. A mortgage payment was due on Fruitlands. Sam May, trustee of Abba's inheritance, wrote to Lane that he would not release the money for the payment. The Consociate Family would have to leave Fruitlands, but for where? Endless talk went on—around the meager fire, between Bronson and Lane in private, between Bronson and Abba in their bedroom.

"Father and Mr. L. had a talk, and father asked us if *we* saw any reason for us to separate," Louisa wrote in her journal on November 20. "Mother wanted to, she is so tired."

Nine days later came her eleventh birthday and Bronson's forty-fifth. Louisa's journal records none of the usual day-long celebrations. The next remaining entry comes on December 10. "Mr. L. was in Boston, and we were glad. In the eve father and mother and Anna and I had a long talk. I was very unhappy, and we all cried. Anna and I cried in bed, and I prayed God to keep us all together."

The crisis had peaked. With Mr. Lane at last absent, Abba had flung down her challenge. Sam May was begging her to leave Bronson and take the children with her. Sam and other friends would provide housing. She *was* leaving; Bronson could come with them or go his own way—alone, or with Charles Lane. The Alcotts were either going to have a normal family life in a normal home, or the marriage was ending. Bronson had to choose.

Bronson, faced with the ultimatum, chose wife and family. The question was settled—forever. Louisa's worst fears would not be realized. But some things were forever changed. Bronson was a Hoper no longer. He was sick in body and in soul. Abba had won a bitter victory.

Lane went to Concord in December and was jailed for not paying taxes. Set loose after someone else paid the debt, he went back to Fruitlands. On Christmas Eve, Bronson went to Boston to attend a convention, leaving Lane behind. He was gone for the rest of the year.

On Christmas Day, Fruitlands was snowbound. Somehow, Abba managed to fill stockings for her girls, and they had also made little gifts for one another. She wrote a poem in Louisa's journal:

> Christmass is here
> Louisa my dear
> Then happy we'll be
> Gladsome and free. . . .

Twice Mr. Lovejoy broke a path through the snow to the old red farmhouse. In the evening the Lovejoy children came over. Abba tried to cheer them all with play and singing.

Anna was still at Cousin Louisa Willis's in Boston. Louisa missed her badly. During Christmas week she wrote a poem for Anna, read Martin Luther, and "wrote in my Imagination Book, and enjoyed it very much. Life is pleasanter than it used to be, and I don't care about dying any more." We can

75

only guess at what had been going through Louisa's mind.

Bronson came back to Fruitlands on New Year's Day, 1844. The Alcotts' course was now set. All ties with the Fruitlands experiment had officially been severed. As soon as they could pack, they would move in with the Lovejoys in nearby Still River, Massachusetts, renting three rooms and kitchen privileges for fifty cents a week. The rent would be paid by Sam May, probably out of Abba's inheritance.

First the hundreds of books must be inventoried and packed. Money for the move was still lacking, so Abba sold her own cloak and some silver that had been given to her by a dear old friend. The Lanes left to join the Shakers, Mr. Lane still complaining that Bronson's enduring love for his wife and family had "blurred his life forever." Abba wrote to her brother Sam, in exhausted triumph, that all Lane's efforts to break up the family had been in vain.

Through that terrible winter of cold and sickness, all that stood between the Alcotts and starvation was thirty-two dollars and the kindness of their neighbors.

Somehow, in the spring, they were able to move again, into half of a nearby house called Brick Ends, for two dollars a month. Bronson made halfhearted attempts at farming, or roamed the country. He was deep in a breakdown and close to madness. Abba was full of anxiety and dread. But they were all together.

In the warmth of spring, life became better for Louisa. She and Anna entered the district school with a lively young teacher named Maria Louisa Chase. She made a good friend, Sophia Gardner, whom May, unable to pronounce "Sophia," renamed "Fire." Classmates began bringing extra food in their lunch buckets to share with Anna and Louisa.

Slowly, life became more normal. Summer brought picnics in haycarts, a glorious celebration of Lizzie's ninth birthday, and plays. Louisa had begun writing thrilling dramas and other theatrical entertainments, which she staged in the house or in the barn. Among the young people of Still River, Louisa was the recognized leader.

Everyone knew the Alcott girls. Anna, quiet and proper, turned into an unexpectedly good dramatic actress whenever she set foot on a stage. Lizzie was serene and cheerful, a born housekeeper whom her sisters called "our little conscience." By the time May was four she was already a charmer with elegant airs. And Louisa—tall as a boy, thin as a beanpole, given to black moods and fits of inspiration—filled life with thunder and lightning and made it magic.

Everyone wanted to be part of Louisa's plays. Abba found a new recruit for Louisa on the Boston coach. Fourteen-year-old Llewellyn Willis was an orphan, distantly related to the Mays. He had been apprenticed to an apothecary, or pharmacist, and was on his way to spend the summer in Still River. Abba took him under her maternal wing, and within a week he was boarding with the Alcotts. He became Louisa's "dear boy," enthusiastic collaborator, and lifelong friend.

The months of the Alcotts' new life were rolling by. There was still no income. Abba was beginning to realize she would have to be the family breadwinner. On November 12 the Alcotts boarded a stagecoach, and after that the wondrous new railroad train, for the journey back to Concord. They were going to take refuge at the Edmund Hosmers' farm.

They were, none of them, the same people who had left for Fruitlands with high hopes and grand illusions. Bronson's spirit was broken, and his golden hair had all turned gray. The marks of suffering were on Abba; she had become cynical and lost all her illusions. And Louisa was about to enter into her true inheritance—the gift of writing.

In 1845 another, more tangible inheritance came through.

Colonel May's estate was finally settled. Sam had managed to work out a settlement with Bronson's creditors. The rest of Abba's legacy was in a trust to be managed by Sam May and a cousin, Sam Sewall. What this meant was that Abba was guaranteed a small but permanent income—enough to keep the wolf away from the door, and to partly provide a house for the door to be attached to.

Emerson found the house for them, not far from his own on the Lexington Road in Concord. It was 145 years old and had only four rooms, but it had nooks and crannies, barns and attics, and an enchanting woodland in the rear. Sam May and Sam Sewall bought it for Abba, and Emerson contributed money to buy the meadowland across the way.

Bronson Alcott had a genius for house and garden design and would have made a wonderful architect or landscaper. He fell to work in a fit of excitement, transforming the old house as he had once transformed Dove Cottage. He named it Hillside.

Hillside sprouted two wings, made by cutting the old wheelwright shop in two and tacking it on the ends. One wing was Bronson's study. The other was for storage and for bathing—Bronson contrived a shower bath out of pails, weights, and pulleys. A large new kitchen was created, and new stairs. The outside gleamed with a coat of olive-green paint. Then Bronson threw himself into farming the meadowland.

Louisa entered her teens that first Hillside autumn.

Some time that autumn, Louisa was deeply moved by an experience she would never forget.

"I had an early run in the woods before the dew was off the grass," she wrote in her journal. "The moss was like velvet, and as I ran under the arches of yellow and red leaves I sang for joy, my heart was so bright and the world so beautiful. I

Norma Johnston

**HILLSIDE, LATER CALLED WAYSIDE. THE WINGS WERE ADDED BY
BRONSON ALCOTT AND THE TOWER STUDY BY NATHANIEL
HAWTHORNE. THE VERANDA WAS ADDED BY THE SUBSEQUENT
OWNERS, PUBLISHER DANIEL LOTHROP AND HIS WIFE,
"MARGARET SIDNEY," AUTHOR OF *FIVE LITTLE PEPPERS.***

stopped at the end of the walk and saw the sunshine out over the wide 'Virginia meadows.'

"It seemed like going through a dark life or grave into heaven beyond. . . . I *felt* God as I never did before, and I prayed in my heart that I might keep that happy sense of nearness in my life." Years later, Louisa herself noted in the margin, "I have."

In March 1846 Louisa achieved one of her greatest dreams—a room of her own.

"It does me good to be alone," she wrote. "My workbasket and desk are by the window, and my closet is full of dried herbs that smell very nice. The door . . . opens into the garden. . . . I can run off to the woods when I like.

"I have made a plan for my life, as I am in my teens, and no more a child. I am old for my age, and don't care much for girl's things. People think I'm wild and queer; but Mother understands and helps me. I have not told any one about my plan; but I'm going to *be* good. I've made so many resolutions, and written sad notes, and cried over my sins, and it doesn't seem to do any good! Now I'm going to *work really*, for I feel a true desire to improve, and be a help and comfort, not a care and sorrow, to my dear mother."

She had found her course, and she never departed from it. Plays and poems and stories poured out of her unconscious. Abba gave Louisa a pen of her own for her fourteenth birthday, along with a poem: "Oh! may this pen your muse inspire. . . ."

Louisa was becoming more and more like her mother. They had the same May temperament, the same passionate loves and hates, the same streak of realism that grounded their visions with practicality. Now they were growing alike in a kind of silent, secret bond to protect Bronson and take care of the family. Louisa adored Abba, admired her, recognized her strengths and talents. Abba gave Louisa the confidence that her own ambitions could come true.

Louisa loved her father also. He had been a creator of magic for her when she was small. Now, as she grew older, she began to understand his genius and his failings, and to protect him fiercely, as her mother did. But Bronson never had the same warmth toward Louisa that he did toward Anna and Lizzie, his favorite daughters. There was always a strange mixture of love and alienation between Bronson and Louisa.

During her teens Louisa found another father figure to worship and fall in love with. It was Mr. Emerson, in the gracious, square white house along the Lexington Road. Ralph Waldo Emerson was a romantic figure. He had adored his young bride, and she had died during their first year of marriage. He had lost other people whom he loved. By middle age, though he had remarried and had children, Emerson was both sociable and remote. A wonderful hero for a thrilling story—and for a teenage girl who was a writer. He was also living proof that a person could be a genius—and a writer—and earn a comfortable living.

Emerson was kind to starry-eyed Louisa. He guided her reading, allowed her to hero-worship, and gave her the run of his library. Most of all, he paid her the high compliment of taking her seriously as a writer and talking to her about writing.

The friendship between Bronson Alcott and Emerson was never the same as it had been before Bronson deserted Emerson and Concord for Lane and Fruitlands. Now Bronson's closest companion was Henry Thoreau. Both were loners, both loved nature and teaching, both were eccentrics. Thoreau became almost the son Bronson never had, and the second love of Louisa's teenage life. He was unable to reciprocate. But he took the Alcott girls and Llewellyn Willis out in his boat on Walden Pond, taught them about Native American lore, and played his flute for them.

Thanks to Emerson, Lousia developed a passion for the works of Goethe, the German romanticist, and Charles Dickens. She could understand Dickens's outrage at poverty and injustice and his lovably eccentric characters. The Alcott girls formed their own Pickwick Club (just as the March girls would, in *Little Women*), wrote their own newspaper, and acted out Dickens's stories.

In Concord, as in Still River, Louisa was the dominant figure among her sisters and among their young friends. Louisa was always the leader in outdoor games and derring-do. But the most popular activity for them all was Louisa's "theatricals." They took many forms, just as professional theater performances did in those days. Some were *tableaux,* or "living pictures"—the curtains would open to show the actors posed, like figures in a store-window display, in scenes from art or thrilling stories. Some were variety programs—a mix of song, dance, musical selections, and dramatic readings. Some were plays—in the nineteenth century plays had four or five acts, and many scenes, with elaborate special effects such as offstage thunder. Louisa was good at writing these, getting ideas from the works of Shakespeare or Sir Walter Scott.

All the sisters worked together on these plays, with help from eager friends such as Llewellyn Willis when allowed. Louisa and Anna made costumes and scenery and played the main roles. Lizzie and May ran errands and did whatever their sisters would permit. What was special about the Alcott plays was the heroines (usually played by Anna; Louisa liked to play men's roles). The typical heroine of the time was a Sleeping Beauty type—pale, helpless, and in need of rescue.

Louisa's heroines had *courage*. They could do brave deeds, sacrifice themselves for those they loved, have high adventures. Sometimes, even, they were—or seemed to be—the villains. Louisa had not read Shakespeare and the ancient Greek playwrights for nothing.

Little Ellen Emerson adored Louisa, who made up "flower fables" for her. Bronson Alcott had repeatedly been refused a teaching post in Concord, but Louisa opened a little school of her own in the Hillside barn. There she taught the Emerson children the arithmetic Charles Lane had taught her, the reading she'd learned from her father, and whatever she remembered from her other teachers. She was very conscious that the time was coming when she would have to "fall to" and help support the family.

Since returning to Concord, Bronson Alcott had not been able to earn any money—not at any work he was willing to accept. By Louisa's fifteenth birthday the Alcotts were in debt again, and the local storekeepers were threatening to cut off credit. Like a miracle, an offer of employment for both Bronson *and* Abba arrived.

A "water-cure house"—a cross between a mountain resort hotel and a nursing home—was being opened in Waterford, Maine. "Sanitariums" like this were popular in the nineteenth century, for poor health was commonplace. With city air polluted from coal fires and factory chimneys, sanitation poor, and today's miracle drugs not yet discovered, consumption (tuberculosis) and pneumonia were rampant. People went to "water-cure houses" to "take the waters" from hot mineral springs via baths or wet-sheet wrappings. Abba was asked to be matron (manager) and Bronson to come along as "preacher and teacher."

All winter Louisa's parents argued over the offer. Abba saw it as heaven-sent. Bronson, maddeningly calm, refused to budge. He did not have a "clear call" within himself and saw no reason to go to work without it.

By the spring of 1848, Abba had had enough. If Bronson would not go to work in Maine, *she* would go without him. She took with her eight-year-old May and Eliza Stearns, a mentally handicapped teenager who had been boarding in the Alcotts' care at Hillside. Anna had already gone to stay with Cousin Lizzie Wells in Walpole, New Hampshire, and was earning money teaching a little summer school. Lizzie and Louisa were left to keep house for Bronson.

In Maine, Abba May Alcott's managerial abilities burst into flower. The work was exhausting, but she was brilliant at it. She was too busy to look after May properly and sent her back to Hillside. Abba was using her talents and making money, but she missed her family deeply. She began having disturbing dreams about them. At the end of three months she resigned her post and went back to Concord with her earnings.

Abba had learned something important during those three months. She had proved to herself that she was capable of earning a living. She knew there were no opportunities in Concord, so as soon as she was home she began "putting out feelers" to friends and relatives in Boston. The Alcotts were going to have to move again—they had been trying to find a buyer for Hillside for over a year—and Abba was convinced that Boston was where they belonged.

The May family swung into action. Aunt Hannah Robie and Aunt Mary May (the wife of Colonel May's brother) were powerful women in Boston. By late October 1848, the wheels were turning. Women of power and influence were secretly putting together a position for Abba. A tenant turned up wanting to rent Hillside. Even Bronson was eager to make the move. He began envisioning all sorts of new opportunities for a "ministry of talking." He was again the Hoper.

On November 17, 1848, the Alcotts boarded the railway car for Boston, the Mays' own city. Louisa was leaving behind her the joys of amateur theatricals, the "room of her own" that opened on the woods, the long hours in Emerson's library, young Ellen Emerson's devotion. In twelve days she would be sixteen, and in her eyes she was no more a child. Ever since Fruitlands she had dreamed of being able to support the family. It was time for her to begin.

TEN

"My Girls Shall Have Trades"

BOSTON AT THE END of the 1840s was like a New Jerusalem, a "city set upon a hill." Church spires sparkled in the sunlight and the gold dome of the statehouse gleamed.

Yet Boston was changing. Brick and stone townhouses were rising on Beacon Hill, on the north side of the Common. Factories and warehouses had gone up near the piers. North Boston, Fort Hill, and the South End (where the Puritans had landed) were turning into slums. Some fifty thousand immigrants had crowded into the city in the past ten years, and the conditions they were living in were frightful.

The May ladies of Boston had persuaded twenty-one other wealthy women, and one male millionaire, to band together and hire Abba Alcott to be their "Missionary to the Poor." She was to visit the poor of the Ward 11 district in the South

End, investigate their needs, and decide how the committee's contributions should be used. She would be paid thirty dollars a month.

Abba became a professional social worker—one of the first ever. She plunged into the task with all her enthusiasm and executive ability. She had been raised to be a good samaritan, and she had experienced poverty and desperate need firsthand.

What she discovered in Ward 11 made the destitution of Fruitlands seem like paradise. The Consociate Family had at least had beds and apples. Here as many as fourteen people slept in a single room, in abandoned warehouses, or on the dirt floors of shanties. These unfortunate immigrants were the poorest of the poor—ignorant, unskilled, illiterate, unwell. Ward 11 and the other slum districts were festering sewers, magnets for disease and crime. For one dauntless woman to try to make a difference was like trying to bail out the ocean with a teaspoon. But Abba tried.

The Alcotts' new home was three rooms and a kitchen in a basement on Dedham Street, a world apart from the comforts of the "May part of town." Abba threw herself into her work, and she didn't limit it only to Ward 11. She was everywhere, pestering officials, begging for more funds, picking her way through dank filthy corridors in her shawl and crinoline and simple bonnet. She worked long hours, and the more she gave of herself, the more was needed.

While she struggled, the rest of the family made do without her. Bronson found a room on West Street, just off the Common, where he could conduct lessons and Conversations. Anna was a live-in governess with one of the May relatives in a nearby suburb. Lizzie and May went to school.

Louisa's job, for the moment, was keeping house. All she could see through the Dedham Street windows as she washed and cooked was a parade of muddy feet passing by. Three nights a week she joined her mother in teaching reading and writing to illiterate black adults. She did all she could to lift the family's spirits and her own, staging family theatricals in the basement kitchen. But she missed her Concord friends and activities, and she was still trying to find a way to earn real money. For the moment, she was needed most at home, a rebellious keeper of pots and pans and broom.

Mrs. James Savage, one of the Alcotts' perpetual benefactors, rescued them from the slum during the summer. Like most wealthy Bostonians, the Savages left the city during hot weather, and their house at 1 Temple Place was available rent-free. The Alcotts moved into it gratefully.

Through most of that hot, silent summer, Bronson had the house to himself. Abba hurried in and out, intent upon her work. She was busy evaluating conditions in Ward 11, studying the latest reports on how to solve the poverty problem, drawing up plans. Daily, for longer and longer hours, she ministered to her clients with the insufficient resources available. Louisa and her sisters often stayed with their more fortunate relatives. Bronson was alone with his pen and with his thoughts.

He began work on what he hoped would be his life's achievement, a book of philosophic "gems" that he called *Tablets*. It was not good for him to be alone. All his life, when caught in a whirlwind of creativity, he became swept away and lost touch with the world outside his head. It happened again now. He became obsessed with his writing and reading, his diagrams and charts. His excitement spiraled into a manic state.

This November he would be fifty years old—more than half a lifetime—and he knew that his greatest triumphs lay behind him. The failure of Fruitlands, the inability to reestablish himself as a respected teacher while in Concord, ate at him. As at Fruitlands, the feverish excitement was followed by exhaustion and withdrawal. Two of his sisters had died; now another followed them. Worse, his younger brother Junius went insane. Bronson became preoccupied again with his conflicting pulls between flesh and spirit.

For the winter of 1849–1850 the Alcotts moved back near Abba's work, at 12 Groton Street. Anna and Louisa were busily making plans to open their own school next year. Lizzie, disappointing her parents, had dropped out of school and took over as the family housekeeper. May was studying with Elizabeth Peabody, who was once more in Abba's good graces.

And Abba? Abba had gone into social work a liberal, sure that learning good organization and the Puritan work ethic would help the poor help themselves out of poverty. By the time the midcentury mark was reached, she had lost her illusions and become a radical. The problems of poverty were too big for *anyone*. What was needed was a change in society itself.

Every month she gave her sponsors a detailed report. She made speeches, and her reports were published in the papers. She had become a public, and political, figure. And she was very angry.

She brought her worst-case clients into her own home. She opened a Relief Office in the Groton Street house. She turned her sarcastic tongue on the ladies of her committee. She was beginning to alienate even her friends.

Louisa was earning two dollars a week doing odd jobs— sewing, cleaning, and laundering. Bronson was close to a total breakdown, but his personal magnetism could still burn brightly. His Conversations had acquired a regular following of young woman admirers.

All the family looked forward to the summer, which they would spend this year in Sam May's house at 88 Atkinson Street. Abba was now handling 200 cases a month, with the constant necessity of saying no to pleas for help. In March she turned in her final report to the missionary committee, and it was a stinger. Among other things, she issued a ringing call for a national program against poverty. Now she was exhausted and depressed.

A cholera epidemic was sweeping through the slums that summer. On Atkinson Street, the Alcotts could feel safe from that.

They did not get cholera. They did get smallpox.

Abba came down with it first, probably from some poor urchins she had invited into the garden to be fed. She was seriously ill. Then, in turn, the disease moved on to the other members of the family—Anna, then Louisa, then May, then Elizabeth, then their father. The girls' cases were light, but Bronson almost died.

It was a " curious time of exile, danger and trouble," Louisa wrote after it was over. All through that long June they saw no doctors and took no drugs; they treated each other with home remedies, rest, and tender nursing. Given the popular treatments of the time (including bleeding, draining the "poisonous" blood from the patient), it was probably the best thing they could have done.

The experience left them all with a terrible awareness of the precariousness of their situation. All this time, the Mays and the Sewalls and the rest of Abba's relatives were pressuring her to leave Bronson or, at the very least, force him to get a job. That was hopeless, Abba knew. Whether she knew just how bad his mental state was is unclear.

They all recovered from the smallpox, and they went on. Abba went into business for herself, opening an "Intelligence

Service," or employment agency for household workers, in the Atkinson Street house.

In the autumn of 1850 the Alcotts and the Intelligence Service had to leave Atkinson Street, and this time they hit rock bottom. Number 50 High Street lay at the cutting edge between Fort Hill, Boston's worst slum, and the better part of town. The worlds of the rich and the very poor confronted each other in the Alcott home, where upper-class Boston came looking for cheap labor, and unskilled labor (most of it female) looked in vain for a living wage. Home workers earned as little as twenty cents a day. The cheapest housing rented for $1.25 a week. Abba herself never earned more than a dollar a day, sometimes as little as a nickel.

Grandmother Anna Alcox came for a visit and was horrified. Even the hardscrabble poverty of Spindle Hill had not been as bad as this!

The United States in 1850 was crying out for change. Two things of major significance were happening. One involved the passage of the Fugitive Slave Law, which was part of a compromise deal that kept slavery out of California. Under the new law, any slave who escaped, even if he reached the free states of the North, was to be hunted down by federal marshals and returned to the owner. Anyone hiding or otherwise helping the runaway was subject to punishment. Boston was a main stop on the Underground Railway, and abolitionists there were outraged.

Another major event was the growth of the women's movement and the demand for equal rights and the power to vote. Female suffrage, it was called. A great convention had been held at Seneca Falls, New York, in 1848, and soon after that Abba Alcott joined the movement. The work she was doing among poor women in the slums showed her the need for women's suffrage—and so did her own life.

While she was active in the movement, Abba organized a petition for women's suffrage that was sent to the Massachusetts State Constitutional Convention. Among the many signatures were those of William Lloyd Garrison, the Reverend Samuel Joseph May, Samuel Sewall, and Amos Bronson Alcott.

Unbeknownst to Abba, Bronson did not just have women's suffrage on his mind that year. One particular woman was constantly in his thoughts, and she wasn't Abba. Ednah Dow Littlehale, who was half his age, had been attending the Conversations regularly for some time. Like Bronson himself, like Margaret Fuller and the other women who had fallen for him, Ednah Littlehale had intelligence and magnetism. She was also spectacularly beautiful. Even Louisa admired her. There had been many women who adored Bronson. This one *he* adored.

Ednah brought Bronson's youth back to him, and his faith in himself. She was for Bronson the one bright spot in two very bleak years. Louisa's journal summary of 1851 reads: "Father trying to talk. Mother had an Intelligence Office. . . . Poor as rats & apparently quite forgotten by every one but the Lord."

In February 1851 a fugitive slave named Shadrach was recaptured in Boston, the first victim of the Fugitive Slave Law. He was rescued that afternoon and whisked away to a Railway stop in Concord. Another slave, Thomas Simms, recaptured in April, was not so lucky. A great protest rally was held, and the Alcotts attended.

"I shall feel horribly ashamed of my country if this thing happens and the slave is taken back," Louisa wrote in her journal. He was.

Ednah and Bronson began taking walks in the Common at dawn nearly every morning. It was much like the friendship between Louisa and Emerson a few years earlier, with two exceptions. Ednah was not a preteen; she was a woman. And Bronson was falling in love, as his ecstatic journal entries showed.

Ednah went to New Hampshire during the summer of 1851. When she returned, the meetings with Bronson began again. Bronson didn't know that his platonic romance was already doomed. While in New Hampshire Ednah had met the famous portrait artist Seth Cheney, a widower in his early forties. By the end of October, Cheney was back in his Boston studio, and Ednah took Bronson to meet him. They met again at a social event at which many celebrities, including Emerson, were guests. Bronson admitted in his journal that he felt out of place. He may have sensed that he had already lost Ednah to the painter. He must have seen the irony in it. Cheney was so very much like Bronson. But the few differences were major. Cheney was successful, wealthy, still handsome, and unmarried.

By Thanksgiving, Bronson had struggled to an inner serenity and a return of his love for Abba. Not the kind of love the two of them had had twenty years before; he knew now that he and Abba could never "lose" themselves in each other as they had both once dreamed. As their letters and journals show, they had discovered that they were two very different people. They had different goals. But in spite of everything, they did love and appreciate each other.

That autumn, Louisa became a published author at last. Her poem "Sunlight" appeared in the September issue of *Peterson's Magazine* under the byline "Flora Fairfield." Such flowery pen names were common in those days.

One poem did not bring instant fame, and Louisa was wise enough to know it. She was writing short stories and trying to sell them to the popular magazines. But she was also tutoring a young invalid, Alice Lovering, at her home on Beacon Street, for which she was paid $40 in 1851. She began recording her yearly earnings in her journal in 1850, reporting $50 for teaching school and $10 for her sewing.

It was not enough. Louisa's journal summary for 1851 goes on: "I go to Dedham as a servant & try it for a month, but get starved & frozen & give it up."

There was a world of bitter experience behind that sentence. Conditions were so bad that when a Dedham clergyman appeared at the Intelligence Office, looking for a companion for his invalid sister, Louisa proposed herself for the position. The position the gentleman described sounded more interesting than sewing. It was a house of wealth and refinement, with books and pictures and a piano. Louisa would be a member of the family, expected only to do the light tasks his sister was too weak to handle.

Louisa had to work harder than that at home. Besides, her pride was the kind that found greater dignity in scrubbing floors than in accepting charity. She set off for Dedham with her three homemade dresses, her aprons and sweeping caps. The position turned out to be not as advertised.

The house had been neglected. Louisa worked hard putting it back in order. The household members were the invalid lady, a nervous little woman; her polite elderly father; and her brother. The brother was the problem. He began at once to harass Louisa with his attentions. After a morning's hard labor she was expected to come into his study and listen to him read aloud or discuss metaphysical philosophy. It was Fruitlands all over again, except that she was now a young woman in her late teens, and his interest was not just philosophical. He bothered her with poetry while she was washing dishes, slipped reproachful notes under her bedroom door.

Finally, in the middle of scrubbing the kitchen floor, Louisa could take no more. She turned on him, brandishing her scrub brush. She had been hired to be his *sister*'s companion, not his!

From then on she was treated like a slave. She had to do all the hard household work—shovel snow, split kindling, bring water from the well. Like Cinderella, she worked from dawn till well into the night. All that kept her going was the thought of the salary to come, and the things she would buy with it for her family.

After seven weeks she could take no more. She handed in her notice and left for the railway station, pushing her trunk before her in a wheelbarrow. The invalid sister had tucked a cheap purse into Louisa's hand as she was leaving. Before she reached the station Louisa's hopes got the better of her. She stopped in the road and looked.

Inside the purse were four one-dollar bills. That was all her pay for nearly two months' hard labor. When she reached home, her outraged parents returned the four dollars for her.

"My girls shall have trades," Abba had vowed, determined they would never find themselves in the situation she had. And sure enough, Louisa could sew, teach, keep house, and nurse. But if she was ever going to provide her mother with a quiet room of her own, let alone get one for herself, it would be through none of those. She had two other talents, Louisa knew, that could bring either feast or famine. She could act, and she could write.

All the family could write, but Louisa alone determined to teach herself how to write in ways for which the public would pay good money. And it was starting. By the end of 1851 she had already sold two stories.

Back in Concord when she was sixteen, Louisa had written a story called "The Rival Painters." Llewellyn Willis took it to the *Olive Branch,* and publisher Thomas Norris had bought it for $5. It would be published anonymously some time in the future. She had written "A Masked Marriage," and sold it for $10 to *Dodge's Literary Museum*. It, like "Sunlight," would be published under a pen name. But she was indeed "learning a trade."

ELEVEN

"Half - Writ Poems, Stories Wild ..."

IN 1852 THE ALCOTTS' LUCK at last began to turn.

Nathaniel Hawthorne, the romantic figure whom young Louisa used to see around the Old Manse, decided to move back again to Concord. He had been away for some time. Now he was the successful author of a scandalous novel Louisa had been devouring, *The Scarlet Letter*. He took a good look at Hillside, up the road from the Emerson house. The place had run down again in the years the Alcotts had been renting it out, but it still had charm.

Bronson had bought Hillside originally with money from Abba's trust fund, plus $500 from Emerson to buy the field across the way. Hawthorne arranged with Abba's executor, her cousin Sam Sewall, to buy Hillside for $1,000, and he paid Emerson $500 for the field. Emerson promptly set up a

97

trust fund for Bronson with his $500, and Sam Sewall put the $1,000 back into Abba's trust.

With the income from the trust added to the small sums Abba and Bronson, Anna and Louisa brought in, they were at last able to rent proper housing. They moved into a brick house at 20 Pinckney Street, on Beacon Hill, not far from many of the May relatives. It was not a very grand house, but it was in the best part of town. From then on, even at their poorest, they never again lived in a slum.

Abba was in her fifties now, putting on weight and growing old. She was sick, exhausted, and discouraged that all her efforts had hardly made a dent in the sufferings of the urban poor. A streak of bitterness and prejudice had crept in that was unlike her. Raised in the Puritan beliefs of ambition, cleanliness, and a faith that if you just worked hard enough you could *make* life better, she was baffled by clients whose condition was so harsh they didn't even see any point in trying. Abba could take no more. She gave up work outside the house forever.

Louisa didn't have that luxury. She was passionately interested in the issues of the day—abolition and women's rights. There were events being held on behalf of both those causes, and she followed them closely when she could. When Harriet Beecher Stowe's abolitionist novel *Uncle Tom's Cabin* came out in 1852, it immediately became a bestseller and one of Louisa's favorite novels. Mrs. Stowe had lived on the border between North and South, her home was a "station" on the Underground Railway, and she knew the evils of slavery firsthand. Her book graphically showed the horrors of black families being torn apart and sold, the Fugitive Slave Law, and the torture and death that could come even to a "good slave" like Uncle Tom, who was portrayed almost as a biblical

LOUISA MAY ALCOTT, C. 1850

saint. Louisa hoped to be able to write like Stowe, who was also writing out of a family's deep financial need.

For now, Louisa and Anna ran a school in their Pinckney Street parlor; Louisa made $75 that year teaching. She kept on sewing (sheets and pillowcases, mostly). And she kept on writing. Abba took in lodgers. The Alcott Sinking Fund, as Louisa called her savings, was slowly growing. Above all else, she wanted the family—especially her mother—to be safe.

The Pinckney Street house had a second-floor parlor where Louisa could put on the plays she wrote. The family played games there or listened while Louisa read aloud. From time to time, some relative would send tickets to a lecture, a play, or a concert. When Louisa walked through the gaslit tiers of the splendid new Music Hall, she forgot her shabby gown in thinking of stories and plays she could weave around this setting. Or of what it would be like to stand herself, Louisa May Alcott, on that stage. . . .

All things must have seemed possible to her at times, especially when "The Rival Painters" was finally published in the *Olive Branch*.

At home the balance of power had shifted. Louisa and Anna were now the breadwinners, and Louisa, although the younger, was the leader. Bronson was once again the peddler of philosophical ideas in his Conversations, but something was happening to him. His ability to think brilliantly and clearly was escaping him. He repeated himself. He became eccentric, becoming engrossed in a study of genetics and getting wild ideas that glorified the Saxon peoples over others.

Bronson was under many strains. His brother Junius, whom he had loved, had been battling insanity. That spring Junius was killed in the machinery of the factory where he worked. The sad letter Anna Alcox wrote telling Bronson of the tragedy hints at Junius's suicide. During the summer, Ednah Littlehale went again to New Hampshire, and while there she and Seth Cheney became engaged. Bronson's romance had come to an end.

Some things about the Alcott-Littlehale-Cheney triangle were remarkable, and show the greatness of character of all three. They were able to remain friends. Cheney the artist did a bas-relief sculpture of Bronson that brings out all his noble qualities. Ednah and Louisa were close, and many years later Ednah became Louisa's first biographer.

In 1853 the Cheneys married and left for Europe. Louisa kept school from January to May. In March an unexpected honor came to Bronson. A group of Harvard Divinity School students invited him to give a series of "Conversations on Modern Life." They were a new generation of listeners, unaffected by the ridicule their elders now heaped on the transcendentalists.

During the summer Louisa went to her May cousins in Leicester, Massachusetts, as a sort of mother's helper. In the fall Anna again left home, this time to teach in a school in Syracuse, New York. This position also came to her through May relatives. But the greatest family achievement was that Bronson was again on the road in a Ministry of Talking.

It happened as a result of the Harvard meetings, and of Emerson admitting Bronson back into intimate friendship. Emerson had gained wealth and fame through his lecture tours and was enthusiastic about the American West, where Nature was still unspoiled. Why shouldn't Bronson Alcott also try his luck on the lecture circuit? Perhaps going as far as the river port of Cincinnati, Ohio, then known as the Gateway to the West?

The tour was a triumph. There were whole new audiences eager to hear Bronson speak about philosophy and education. Exultantly, Bronson sent $150 home to Abba. Bronson and Abba's marriage was back on a sure footing. They were writing love letters to each other again, just as in the early years. But now *she* had the power—in the couple, and in the family. *He* had been transformed into a stooped, gentle, old philosopher. Bronson Alcott had found peace at last.

Louisa came from a line of Puritans who understood the biblical story of Jacob wrestling with the angel: "I will not let thee go until thou bless me." She poured all her experiences in Dedham into a story, "How I Went out to Service." Then she gathered her courage and went to the Old Corner Bookstore, where publisher James T. Fields held court in a little room in the rear. She waited while the publisher read her manuscript, a difficult ordeal for any author. At last the great Fields looked up at her paternally.

"Stick to your teaching, Miss Alcott," he said. "You can't write."

Even though not yet twenty, Louisa would not—could not—accept this. She *would* write. And she *would* sell to James T. Fields!

In February 1854, Bronson came home from his lecture tour. Louisa never forgot the moment. He arrived late at night, rousing his womenfolk out of bed. Abba flew down the stairs in her nightgown, a big nightcap and an old jacket as protection against the cold. Straight into Bronson's arms she ran, crying out in ringing tones, "My husband!"

Bronson was hungry, tired, and cold, and he brought only one dollar home with him. His overcoat had been stolen, and he had had to buy a shawl. Traveling had been costly. But he had opened the way, he said. Another year he would do better.

"I call that doing *very well*," Abba said, and she kissed him.

Louisa always remembered the look that passed between them.

Bronson's tour of the West had given him a firsthand look at what had become "a country divided." The causes of that division, which had been festering ever since the days of the Constitutional Convention nearly seventy years earlier, were slavery and states' rights. They had become one issue: the right of a state (or territory) to decide for itself whether it would be slave or free.

In Boston the Reverend Theodore Parker was a leader of abolitionist resistance. As far back as 1846 he had helped organize, and become chairman of, a secret society called the Committee of Vigilance, which protected runaway slaves. Bronson Alcott had become a member as soon as the family returned to Boston. Theodore was a brilliant and respected preacher, and he and his wife became good friends with Louisa. The Committee of Vigilance had had one success, the rescue of the slave Shadrach. It had failed to rescue the slave Thomas Simms.

In the spring of 1854 Senator Stephen A. Douglas's Kansas-Nebraska Act, another proslavery compromise, was about to come to a vote in Congress. The Committee of Vigilance was aroused. So was President Franklin Pierce, who was trying to hold the country together through conciliation. The government was determined to break Boston's abolitionist resistance, and in May the inevitable clash occurred.

Federal marshals seized runaway slave Anthony Burns in the streets of Boston. The president ordered Burns returned to his owner at any cost and promised army units to back up the action. On Wednesday, May 24, Burns was hustled into the Boston courthouse to face the wrath of his former owner and the U.S. government.

Word did not leak out to the Committee of Vigilance until the next day. Its members were at once in conflict over a course of action. Stage a dramatic attempt to seize Burns by force? Or pursue his release through the courts? Basically they were without a leader. Theodore Parker could inspire and serve, but he could not command.

They needed Thomas Wentworth Higginson, the thirty-year-old Unitarian minister who had masterminded the attempt to rescue Thomas Simms. Higginson was living in Worcester, some miles west of Still River. The man sent to get him was his friend Bronson Alcott.

Bronson reached Worcester on Friday evening. The next morning the two men were on the train for Boston. Historical records grow vague from then on. What is known is that the Committee of Vigilance was unable to agree on a plan, and Higginson put together one of his own. He rallied some other abolitionist agitators, including Lewis Hayden, leader of Boston's black abolitionist group. They sent out a call for a mass protest meeting at Faneuil Hall that evening. The idea was that agitators planted in the crowd would cry out for a "citizens' army" which, thus mobilized, would storm the courthouse a few blocks away. Inside they would find Higginson, Hayden, and other conspirators who would lead the charge to rescue Burns and carry him away to freedom.

It was a splendid plan, calling for perfect coordination. By seven in the evening, crowds were pouring into Faneuil Hall. So many hundreds turned out that the result was chaos.

Higginson, with the dozen axes he had bought for battering down doors, sneaked off to the courthouse with his co-conspirators. They found all in silence, lights on inside, and the east door still open. If only the "citizens' army" were already there! But it wasn't. Higginson hesitated. A sheriff came out, stared at Higginson, and slammed the door in his face.

At last a few stragglers appeared. Higginson and a black colleague attacked the west door. It sprang open.

Inside was an army of policemen swinging clubs. At some point someone fired a shot. A mob battle broke out. At its end, Higginson was outside, badly beaten about the head. And a sheriff was dead.

The rest of the "citizens' army"—smaller than Higginson had hoped for—had arrived. Police moved among them, making arrests, and they retreated. Higginson stood in the doorway, with a bloodied face. "Ye cowards, will ye desert us now?" he cried.

Silence. Then one man answered; with his feet, not with his words. Bronson Alcott, his shoulder-length silver hair shining in the light that poured out of the courthouse, moved forward. Cane in hand, utterly serene, he walked up the steps and looked inside. The crowd watched and waited as though under a spell. Bronson looked at the sheriff, lying dead and bathed in blood. At the army of marshals with their weapons drawn. Another shot rang out inside the building.

To proceed would have caused many deaths. All hope of rescuing Anthony Burns was already gone. In fearless calm and absolute sanity, Bronson did the one right thing. He stood, motionless, taking it all in while the crowd's collective breath seemed stopped. Then, slowly, as though he were taking a stroll through the Common, he turned and walked away.

Bronson Alcott had saved Boston from a bloody riot. It was his finest hour.

Anthony Burns was taken back to the South at a cost to the government of $100,000. A few months later, abolitionists raised money to free him and send him to divinity school at Oberlin College. Slavery went on.

As heat closed in on Boston that summer, Louisa was able to visit Uncle Sam and Aunt Lucretia May in Syracuse. Anna was already there as governess in the Charles Sedgwick family. Louisa was working hard on her writing. She was deliberately trying to teach herself to write the kind of stories the *Saturday Evening Gazette* would publish. She had always known how to concoct hair-raising adventures about knights in shining armor and exotic places. Now she began plotting stories that would appeal to modern women like herself and her mother, stories that blended reality and romance, drama and humor.

In November, "The Rival Prima Donnas," a comic tale inspired by her visits to the Music Hall, appeared in the *Saturday Evening Gazette*. And a week before Christmas, an even more important professional turning point occurred. Back in Concord, Louisa had had fun writing a group of fables, with flowers for characters, for Ellen Emerson. She had collected them into book form and polished them, and on December 19, 1854, they became Louisa May Alcott's first published book. There was no pseudonym or disguise via initials this time. Her full name stood out proudly, for all the world and the family's critics to see.

"Dear Mother," Louisa wrote. "Into your Christmas stocking I have put my 'first-born,' knowing that you will accept it with all its faults. . . . Whatever beauty or poetry is to be found in my little book is owing to your interest in and encouragement of all my efforts from the first to the last, and if ever I can do anything to be proud of, my greatest happiness will be that I can thank you for that, as I may do for all the good there is in me."

Abba somehow scraped together enough money to buy Louisa a good desk. A professional writer needed one.

TWELVE

"I've Begun to Live"

"I AM IN THE GARRET with my papers round me, and a pile of apples to eat while I write my journal, plan stories, and enjoy the patter of rain on the roof, in peace and quiet," Louisa wrote in her journal in April of 1855. "Being behind-hand, as usual, I'll make note of the main events up to date, for I don't waste ink in poetry and pages of rubbish now. I've begun to *live,* and have no time for sentimental musing. . . . My book came out; and people began to think that topsey-turvey Louisa would amount to something after all, since she could do so well as housemaid, teacher, seamstress, and story-teller. Perhaps she may."

She had had a busy winter, and had earned $50 for her sewing, $50 for three months' teaching, and $20 for stories. Louisa was finding she could sell any number of stories if she would settle for $5 or $10 apiece. She hoped to do better. She had been to hear lectures on medieval history and to hear Boston poet James Russell Lowell speak on English poetry. She was also having an active social life—as active as her work schedule and her limited wardrobe would permit—for she had many friends and relatives in Boston. She was becoming especially close to Hamilton Willis, the son of Abba's sister Elizabeth, and his wife. Mrs. Willis's name was also Louisa, but the family called her Lu.

Hamilton introduced Louisa to Thomas R. Barry, the manager of the Boston Theatre. Barry showed interest in producing a stage version of Louisa's "Rival Prima Donnas" and told her she could have two free tickets to performances at his theater any time she liked. Both those things filled her with joy.

The Alcotts' summer plans were unsettled. Bronson wanted to go back to England ("Not a wise idea, I think," Louisa noted). Probably 20 Pinckney Street would continue to be home base, and Louisa and Anna would go off as governesses again. In the end they all went to New Hampshire.

All the May relatives seemed to invest in real estate. Ben Willis, Hamilton's father, owned several houses in Walpole, New Hampshire, on the Connecticut River at the Vermont border. The small village was a fashionable summer resort and artists' colony. When Hamilton and Lu invited Louisa to spend the summer there, Louisa was overjoyed. She went in June. In July the others followed her, living rent-free in one of Uncle Ben's houses.

Louisa was welcomed enthusiastically into the Walpole Amateur Dramatic Company. She was a professional writer, she was wonderful at creating costumes and sets and special effects, and she was so funny! She brought down the house playing comic character roles. The ovations from the audience were very sweet. It was a wonderful summer; a time free of worries.

With the coming of autumn, decisions had to be made. Bronson and Abba were happy in Walpole, and they could live on there rent-free if they wished. Anna was offered a teaching post at "the great idiot asylum" in Syracuse, New York. Given the language of the time, that could have meant an insane asylum, a home for the mentally retarded, or both. Anna hated the thought, but the money was needed, and she would be near Uncle Sam and Aunt Lucretia, so she went. She continued to teach there for several years.

Summer in Walpole had been great fun, but Louisa had already discovered some truths about herself. She was a city person. Much as she adored running in the woods and climbing trees, she needed the excitement of the city and its museums, theaters, libraries, and concert halls. She also found it impossible to concentrate on writing when family life swirled around her. It was time for her to be off on her own.

In November, with her trunk of homemade clothes and hand-me-downs from Hamilton's sister Lizzie Wells, her manuscripts, and her $20 from the *Gazette,* Louisa set off alone in the rain for Boston.

Her Sewall cousins welcomed her into their home at 98 Chestnut Street on Beacon Hill. It was a good winter. Boston was full of cultural treats. Louisa heard the celebrated English novelist William Makepeace Thackeray, Dickens's closest rival, speak. She heard author George William Curtis lecture on "Contemporaneous English Fiction." She went to the theater twice a week, thanks to Mr. Barry's passes, and saw the great tragedian Edwin Forrest.

"After being on the stage & seeing more nearly the tinsel & brass of actor life, (much as I should love to be a big star *if* I could,) I have come to the conclusion that its not worth trying for at the expense of health & peace of mind," Louisa wrote her father. She was a voluminous letter-writer.

Louisa may have given up dreams of an acting career but not of becoming a playwright. Her adaptation of "The Rival Prima Donnas" was now in producer Thomas Barry's hands.

Louisa was also reviewing books for a newspaper and sewing for many relatives and friends. She probably took in both "straight sewing" (bed, bath, and table linens) and "fine sewing" (alterations and accessories). For years now Louisa had been the family dressmaker or *re*maker, retrimming bonnets and restyling Lizzie Wells's and Mrs. Savage's hand-me-downs for her mother and her sisters. Women's clothes in the 1850s were beautiful, for the horsehair crinoline had recently been invented. Skirts with two or three tiers of flounces swayed like full-blown flowers beneath tiny waists. Shoulders sloped; sleeves were full at the bottom and worn with delicate lace-trimmed undersleeves.

In the peace of her upstairs bedroom at 98 Chestnut Street, Louisa wrote. Stories poured from her in a steady stream, and she was planning future full-length books. She had a host of material to draw upon. "Write about what you know," beginning authors are always told. Louisa knew about a great deal.

She had her voracious reading, courtesy of both her parents. She had her Puritan heritage, with its belief in perseverance and the work ethic. She had a unique combination of personal experiences, not all pleasant but all worth telling. She had her gift for drama—she could bring scenes to life and evoke strong emotions in her readers.

And there were all the things she had read about, heard about, or witnessed within her family: Suicide and suicide attempts. Insanity. Deaths in childbirth, and stillborn children. All-consuming loves. Passion—for a cause, or for a person. The victimization of women, and the power of a woman's fury. She had gone without food and clothing. She knew the evils of festering slums, and the horrors of slavery. Many authors were writing melodramas about these subjects; Louisa had lived with them. Gradually the prices she received for her stories began to go up.

Louisa was famous enough for the *Gazette* to put up "great yellow placards" advertising her story in a current issue. "[P]eople like the tales, and ask who wrote them," she recorded. J. M. Field of the Mobile Theatre accepted *The Rival Prima Donnas* for production after Mr. Barry turned it down. In between writing, always, was the sewing. One order was for a dozen sheets and pillowcases, two dozen handkerchiefs, and half a dozen fine cambric neckties. Louisa had to sew all night to complete them on time. At least she could plot stories while she worked.

In May, Anna came to Boston on her way from Syracuse to Walpole. She had been unhappy and homesick at the Syracuse asylum; now she was sick and worn out, and Louisa worried over her. They both looked forward to the breezes and pleasures of Walpole.

What they found there was a major crisis.

Abba, being Abba, had taken an interest in the needy poor of Walpole. She had discovered a family living in squalor above a cellar in which pigs had been kept. The children had fallen sick. The landlord refused to clean the place until Abba threatened a lawsuit. Abba, of course, had proceeded to nurse the children.

What they were suffering from turned out to be scarlatina—scarlet fever. This is a streptococcal infection, caused by the same bacteria as strep throat. In the days before the discovery of penicillin, it was a very dangerous disease. By the time Louisa reached Walpole, both Lizzie and May had come down with the disease. May responded to the treatment recommended in Abba's medical book, but Elizabeth was terribly ill. Like most childhood diseases, it is more serious for adults. Elizabeth was having her twenty-first birthday that June.

All through that anxious summer she lay ill as her mother and sisters nursed her tenderly. The swollen glands and sore throat went away; the high fever broke at last and the rash faded. But Lizzie's once round and rosy cheeks were sunken, her face was pale, and she had lost all brightness and appetite.

Elizabeth was uppermost on Louisa's mind all summer, and remained there as the family broke up in the fall. Anna was determined to go back to her asylum work, much as she hated it, for she was well liked there and the pay was good. Bronson left for a speaking tour of New York, Philadelphia, and Boston, with a visit to poet Walt Whitman on his schedule. In October, Louisa set off for Boston. This year she was leaving the shelter of her relatives for life in Mrs. David Reed's great boardinghouse at 34 Chauncy Street.

Louisa had only been able to write one story a month during the summer, but she had plans for more. The *Saturday Evening Gazette* had promised her $10 a story, double her earlier rate. A skyparlor at Mrs. Reed's would cost $3 a week with board and fire. Mr. Reed was publisher of the *Christian Gazette,* so there was bound to be good company and conversation. All the May relatives had promised sewing work. There was also the chance of being governess to Alice Lovering. Louisa was ready to "force the world" again.

"I don't often pray in words; but when I set out that day . . . my heart was full, and I said to the Lord, 'Help us all, and keep us for one another,' as I never said it before," she wrote.

The pie-shaped skyparlor was cozy, and Louisa found her fellow boarders amusing. As always, she was looking for characters for stories, and taking everything in from her corner. Another even more inspiring corner was soon offered. Theodore Parker and his wife held Sunday-evening gatherings at their home at 1 Exeter Place. All the New England intellectual lions, people like William Lloyd Garrison and Julia Ward Howe, made a point of attending when they were in town. Bronson Alcott's author-daughter was honored to be a mouse among these giants. The Parkers took Louisa under their wing, and listening to the kindly minister's wisdom always helped her.

The governess job at the Loverings fell through. Louisa hustled around and lined up additional sewing. Winter set in, much like the one before, offering cultural excitement, hard work, and good talk. In mid-November, sixteen-year-old May arrived at 34 Chauncy Street, on her way to spend the winter with Aunt Louisa May Bond, Grandfather May's adopted daughter. Mrs. Bond had offered to provide May with drawing lessons, for May showed considerable talent, although her anatomical mistakes often made her family laugh.

The Willises took Louisa to plays and operas; Cousin Lu gave Louisa a scarlet crepe shawl to wear in place of her old shabby cloak. Louisa made it all come vividly to life in her letters to Anna and her parents. She always had the ability to twist the hardest experiences into something funny. But in her annual birthday letter to her father she confessed, "I sat alone in my room, with the snow falling fast outside, and a few tears in (for birthdays are dismal times to me)." That November 29, Louisa was twenty-four and Bronson fifty-seven.

Christmastime found Louisa feeling low, for the family seemed very far away and the *Gazette* editor had presented her with the Christmas surprise of a story rejection. She returned to 34 Chauncy Street on Christmas Eve, feeling very blue, to find a box of gifts and letters from Walpole that made her laugh and cry at once. Then Hamilton and Lu Willis scooped her up for Christmas Eve. Not until she was back by the fire in her skyparlor did Louisa open the gift they had pressed on her at the last moment.

It was a small package, and Louisa expected to find a "set of muslins"—undersleeves and collar, a popular gift. Instead the package contained yards of silk, "one stripe bronze & black & one of silvery grey," with Lu's promise to have it made up "in great style." At last Louisa would have the silk gown she had coveted for so long! On New Year's Eve, Louisa went to two parties, proudly wearing the new silk gown. "I felt as if all the Hancocks and Quincys beheld me," she recorded.

She had sold six stories in 1856, including the one the *Gazette* editor had turned down. Her father had earned $300 on his lecture tour "and more to come."

She was entering the new year with high hopes, although she wrote Anna cautiously that "the play *may* come out and I *may* become a woman of wealth." The Loverings had asked her to come as governess again. She was now teaching all three children, as well as taking care of Alice. "[H]ard work, but I can do it," Louisa concluded.

At the end of May, Louisa went to Walpole, stopping for a visit with the Emersons on her way. She had "done what I planned,—supported myself, written eight stories, taught four months, earned a hundred dollars, and sent money home."

It was a joyous reunion in New Hampshire, for Anna returned also and May was already there. But a dark shadow had fallen over the household. Louisa, coming back after half a year's absence, could see it clearly. Elizabeth was terribly frail. She had never really recovered from the scarlet fever, and the long cold winter, hemmed in with ten-foot snow-drifts, had been too much for her. Looking at her, Louisa felt terribly afraid that she might just "slip away."

In July Bronson's mother came to visit, a sweet old lady with white whiskers and a country woman's pipe. The stories she told of Spindle Hill illumined much about Bronson for Louisa. She began planning a story about her "Pathetic Family," as she called it.

The August heat set in. Abba took Elizabeth to the seashore in the hope of restoring some color to her cheeks. Bronson made up his mind to move back to Concord. He needed to be near Emerson again. By September an old house between Emerson's home and Hillside (now called Wayside) had been bought with Abba's money. Abba herself was in Boston with Elizabeth, probably with relatives and possibly consulting doctors. Anna and Louisa broke up the Walpole house and shipped the family belongings back to Concord. It would be months before the new house, which Bronson named Orchard House, would be ready for occupancy.

In the meantime, "home" would be half a house on Bedford Street, Concord, right behind the town hall. Concord was and is a pretty village, straight out of a Christmas card or the Currier and Ives etchings that were wildly popular in the midnineteenth century. Bronson was in walking distance of all his friends. Orchard House was a fine house, suited for gracious living, with grounds that Bronson looked forward to landscaping. Louisa and Anna were busy with work and lives of their own. May was becoming a young lady of talent and great charm. Everything could have been so wonderful. But the great shadow lay across it all.

Elizabeth was dying. The awareness was slowly sinking in on her sisters and parents as the days went by. Louisa, and probably Anna, realized it first because they lived elsewhere and could see the deep changes each time they returned.

What exactly was wrong with Elizabeth has never been proved. Her decline began with the scarlet fever, which has potential side effects. One is rheumatic fever and heart damage. Another is kidney damage. Elizabeth probably also had consumption (tuberculosis); that and pneumonia were two of the main causes of death in the nineteenth century. She may have also sustained unrecognized health damage from her life at Fruitlands and in the Boston slums.

She became weak and frail. She couldn't eat. She couldn't sleep; she had wracking coughs; she was in much pain. She remained, as she had always been, the "angel in the house," as Louisa referred to her in her journal—patient, quiet, cheerful.

Louisa and Anna both gave up all thought of work and life elsewhere to stay in Concord to be near her. They fixed up a nice room in the Bedford Street house for Elizabeth and hoped against hope. In November, Bronson left on a lecture tour, taking his mother back to Spindle Hill on his way. The Concord home was a household of women.

Louisa's twenty-fifth birthday came and went. She was feeling her "quarter of a century rather heavy on my shoulders just now. I lead two lives."

One of them was "gay with plays." Franklin B. Sanborn, who as a tall young undergraduate had heard Bronson speak at Harvard, was now (thanks to Emerson) running a school in Concord. Like Louisa and Anna, he loved the theater. They succeeded in getting a stage put up in the vestry of the Unitarian church and put on a "Series of Dramatic Entertainments." Anna played romantic roles opposite John Bridge Pratt, a kind, quiet young man who lived at his family's farm, Pickle Roost. Louisa played Sophia Tetterby in an adapta-

ELIZABETH SEWALL ALCOTT, C. 1855

Nancy Hill-Joroff

ABBA MAY ALCOTT ("MAY")

tion of Dickens's *The Haunted Man* to the Dolphus Tetterby of fifteen-year-old Alf Whitman. John became Anna's beau, and forever after Alf Whitman was one of Louisa's "dear boys," her "Dearest Dolphus."

Much as Louisa loved the theater, her heart wasn't in her acting that winter. It was in Elizabeth's sickroom. Elizabeth loved to watch her sisters get ready to do shows, so they were doing shows. Elizabeth loved to have Louisa with her, so Louisa was there, all night, every night, ready to stoke the fire, talk, or just be near. Elizabeth felt stronger when Louisa was there.

By New Year's Day, 1858, Elizabeth was much worse. Abba decided to go to Boston to consult Dr. Christian Geist about Elizabeth's terrible cough. One week later, Dr. Geist came to Concord and for the first time told the anxious women, "I cannot give you much hope."

On January 23, 1859, Bronson came home from his lecture tour to help his daughter die.

THIRTEEN

" Apple Slump "

IT WAS CHARACTERISTIC of Bronson and his Puritan heritage that he thought it important to tell Elizabeth the truth and ask her whether her soul was right with God. Lizzie said that it was, and that she was glad to know she was going to "get well." Remaining as cheerful as they could, they all began to make preparations.

Bronson's only son had had to be buried in his in-laws' plot in Boston. But Bronson's home and heart were in Concord now. For his daughter, and for them all when their time came, he bought a plot in Sleepy Hollow Cemetery. Elizabeth herself picked out the spot where she wished to lie.

The plays were given up. Anna took over the housekeeping, so Abba and Louisa could spend all their time with Elizabeth. "Sad, quiet days in her room, and strange nights keeping up the fire and watching the dear little shadow try to wile [sic] away the long sleepless hours without troubling me. She sews, reads, sings softly, and lies looking at the fire,—so sweet and patient and so worn, my heart is broken."

In February of 1858, the weather was mild. Elizabeth rested more comfortably, and her family dared to hope. But she was slowly slipping away like a tide going out to sea. She loved to drop small homemade presents out the window for children passing by to find.

By the first week in March, the needle had become "too heavy" for Elizabeth to hold. She folded her work carefully and put it away forever. She divided her possessions among her family. She had been receiving ether to help her almost constant pain. By the first weekend in March the pain was so intense that she cried out constantly for the ether, but it had lost all its effect. During the next week they all knew the end was near. One day Elizabeth was sure that it had come. She called them all together, kissed their hands, and asked to be held in her father's arms. But she did not die.

All through Saturday, March 13, Elizabeth lingered, in great pain and crying out for help they could not give. At last she slept. At midnight, she awoke, saying, "Now I'm comfortable and so happy." Soon after that she became unconscious. The hours of the night ticked by. At 3:00 A.M. Elizabeth opened her eyes again for a moment, fully aware, unable to speak. Her eyes were beautiful, Louisa would remember. One last look around, and she was gone. It was a few hours before Sunday dawn.

A curious thing happened a few moments after Elizabeth took her last breath. Louisa and her mother were sitting in silence, keeping watch. Suddenly Louisa saw a light mist rise from Elizabeth's body, float upward, and vanish into air. Abba's eyes followed Louisa's. "What did you see?" Louisa asked her mother softly, and Abba described exactly what

Louisa had seen. Dr. Geist, who was also in the room, confirmed it, saying that it was the life leaving the body.

When morning came Elizabeth's mother and sisters dressed her for the last time in her usual cap and gown—a cap because, during her illness and its treatment, all her pretty hair had fallen out. Elizabeth had been twenty-three, but suffering had given her the body of a worn woman of forty.

They buried her the next day where she had asked to lie. None of the Boston relatives and friends were sent for. It was just Ralph Waldo Emerson, Henry Thoreau, Frank Sanborn, and Anna's beau John Pratt who carried her, as Louisa put it, "from her old home to the new." Dr. Huntington, the local minister, read the chapel service, and they all sang Elizabeth's favorite hymn.

A week later Louisa was able to write Cousin Lizzie Wells the sad news. "[O]ur Lizzie is *well* at last, not in this world but another where I hope she will find nothing but rest from her long suffering. . . . We longed for dear Uncle Sam or Mr. Parker. . . . But Uncle was too far away & Parker sick."

For two years Elizabeth had suffered patiently. "[W]e cannot wish her back, but the house is very strange & poor. Mother sits in the empty chamber trying to believe that she shall never hear Lizzie's voice again," Louisa told her cousin, writing in the numb calm that follows tragedy. She could have been speaking of herself. Anna was Louisa's closest companion, May would become her protegé, but quiet Elizabeth had been bonded to Louisa's heart in ways no one would realize for another ten years.

With Elizabeth gone the Alcotts were drifting, for their lives had been put on hold during the past few months. Orchard House was still not ready for occupancy. In April they moved back into one wing of their old home, Hillside, now Nathaniel Hawthorne's Wayside. Elizabeth Peabody's brother (Hawthorne's brother-in-law) was living there while Hawthorne was a U.S. consul in England. The Alcott household was now just Bronson, Abba, and Louisa. May was in Boston studying art. Anna was staying at the Pratt farm, Pickle Roost. In the old house Elizabeth seemed nearer and dearer to Louisa than ever before. "Death never seemed terrible to me," she wrote in her journal, "and now is beautiful; so I cannot fear it, but find it friendly and wonderful."

On the seventh of April, Anna and John Pratt walked into Wayside hand in hand with the news that they were engaged. The family must have seen this was coming, for Anna and John had been playing lovers in Concord Dramatic Society theatricals with remarkable realism. They all liked John Pratt, but the news struck Louisa like a blow. She had lost one sister; now she would lose another. May was already managing to fly away. The old house, Concord, and the small-town atmosphere seemed to be closing like a trap around Louisa.

In June she escaped to Boston and her Willis cousins. She saw Charlotte Cushman act and at once had what she called a "stagestruck fit." Her old friend Thomas Barry agreed to take her on as an actress, playing the role of Widow Pottle that Louisa had often performed in amateur theatricals. It was all a deep secret. Then Mr. Barry broke his leg and the plan was given up. When Louisa's "dear, respectable relations" found out what she had planned to do, they were horrified. She didn't tell them she meant to try again. She was looking for a new life, now that the old one was so changed.

In July the move to Orchard House took place. "We won't move again for twenty years if I can help it," Louisa vowed. But she wasn't referring to herself. By October she had escaped back to Boston on her "usual hunt for employment."

With Anna getting ready for her wedding and May studying art, she was the only breadwinner in the family. She stayed with the Sewalls at 98 Chestnut Street. At first no work surfaced, and Louisa struggled with despair. Mr. Parker's sermon on "Laborious Young Women" put starch in her spine.

What he was saying was good common sense: Trust others to help you, let them do it, and don't be too proud to ask. Take whatever work is offered until what you really want comes along. Once Louisa put this advice into practice, two things *did* come. The first was an inquiry from the Loverings. Would Miss Alcott return to teach Alice *if* they decided to have Alice study at home this winter? Louisa promptly said yes. The next day she was offered a definite job sewing ten hours a day at the Girls' Reform School in Lancaster, Massachusetts. Remembering Mr. Parker's sermon, Louisa accepted—providing the post with the Loverings did not come through. That evening, to her relief, it did.

"I am fixed for the winter and my cares over," Louisa wrote, adding, "Thank the Lord!"

Now that there was income coming in, she moved back into Mrs. Reed's boardinghouse. It wasn't income easily earned. Alice Lovering, Louisa admitted to Alf Whitman, was "a demonic little girl who *dont* digest her food & *does* rave & tear & scold & screech like an insane cherubim. For the sum of two hundred & fifty dollars a year I'm expected to keep the sweet angel happy" and teach her whatever Alice's health (and temper) would permit. But Mrs. Lovering was kind and willing to spend money on Alice's amusement.

In the evenings Louisa looked for fun and found it. The fall theater and lecture season was getting underway. So were private theatricals. Louisa told Alf Whitman she was going to play Edith Granger, "a vast tragic style of female which I shall murder most cheerfully," in a production of Dickens's *Dombey and Son*.

Her twenty-sixth birthday came. The year almost ended had brought the family's first death and first engagement. Both had changed her. She was learning to manage her moods alone, because she felt Abba was too worn out to be burdened with them. In her sorrow she had come nearer to God. She felt better able to write and able to write better. "I hope I shall yet do my great book, for that seems to be my work, and I am growing up to it," she wrote thoughtfully.

In December, May moved in with Louisa, studying drawing under Salisbury Tuckerman (one of Bronson's old Temple School pupils) at the School of Design. Winter brought skating and other winter excitements. May and Louisa went back to Concord for the Christmas holidays. Elizabeth was missing, and John Pratt's teenage brother was dying. To cheer him, the Pratts and Alcotts and their friends threw themselves into making this the liveliest celebration ever. At a production of *The Jacobites* in the Pickle Roost kitchen, Louisa played Major Murray and disgraced herself with great glee, scrambling her lines to the audience's delight. Only John and Anna, playing young lovers, managed to produce realistic acting.

Thanks to the Loverings, Louisa's finances were looking up. She was able to buy a secondhand carpet and bonnet for Anna, shoes and stockings for herself, and put money into the Alcott sinking fund. "No more sewing or going to service for a living, thank the Lord!" she wrote in her journal at year's end.

January of 1859 found Abba ill. Louisa returned to Concord for a week to nurse her and wondered whether she should make nursing her life's work. She had a gift for it; Elizabeth, Lu Willis (who was an asthmatic), and Abba all

126

had said so. Of course, nursing was not a real occupation—at any rate not for a respectable woman. But there were always friends and relatives in need of care from a lady they could trust. Louisa liked nursing. If writing or acting fell through she might try it, she wrote in her journal.

The months went by in a whirl of work and writing, plays and dancing and winter sports. Louisa was practically commuting back and forth between Boston and Concord. Her story "Mark Field's Mistake" appeared in the *Gazette* in March. It was a big success and highly praised. She wrote a sequel, "Mark Field's Success," and had "a queer time over it, getting up at night to write it, being too full to sleep."

In April, Bronson was asked to become superintendent of the Concord school system, and Louisa rejoiced. There was another reason for rejoicing: May had finished her term at the School of Design with high praise. The Loverings had left Boston for a summer of travel, so Louisa was free, with money in her pocket. Louisa and May went back to Concord to see how life in Orchard House was progressing.

The old brown house was truly beautiful. Bronson had been reading the latest theories on decorating and environmental landscaping, and he had taken a large hand in the arrangements of Orchard House inside and out. In contrast to most homes of the era, Orchard House was light and airy, for Bronson made sure the sunlight could pour in. There was a large parlor, with window seats, a stylish mahogany sofa tufted in black horsehair, a center table, and a piano. Through a wide doorway—a suitable "stage opening" for Alcott plays—was the dining room, with Elizabeth's piano and all the treasured May china, with its wide green band and rings of gold and a gold *M* in the center. There was a downstairs study for Bronson and a good large kitchen. Upstairs they all had rooms of their own. May busily ornamented walls and

Norma Johnston

ORCHARD HOUSE, SETTING FOR *LITTLE WOMEN*

mantels with her artwork. She painted an owl over Louisa's bedroom fireplace, symbol of the goddess of wisdom and of Louisa's "owling about."

Orchard House was now the Alcott family homestead, but Louisa herself knew it would never be her home. She knew she needed city life, and she needed a home of her own. That was something almost unheard of for an unmarried woman at that time. Marriage was the dividing line in people's minds between girlhood and adulthood (a concept that was the origin of the term *old maid*). In the same way, a boy became a man when he was able to support a family (that was the reason that Colonel May had frowned upon Bronson as a husband for his daughter). But Louisa was already devising her own pattern. Her own place, and privacy for writing, in the city from fall through spring. Family life in the country when the weather was hot.

Back and forth Louisa went in 1859—Boston to Concord, Concord to Boston. In May Lu Willis was ill, and Louisa nursed her. One day Louisa walked from Concord to Boston—twenty miles in five hours—and went to a party in the evening!

In May, also, Concord turned out to hear an abolitionist celebrity speak at the Town Hall. Captain John "Osawa-tomie" Brown of Connecticut was as visionary as Bronson Alcott, as fanatic as Charles Lane. His dream was to spearhead a slave rebellion that would invade Missouri, wipe out the old slave system and national compromises, and in some way create a "new" United States. He even went so far as to draw up a draft of a new constitution. Concord listened, and was filled with abolitionist zeal.

That summer, Louisa took two children in to board and teach. In September Concord hosted the great encampment of the Massachusetts State Militia. The possibility of civil war was looming large in everybody's mind. "I can't fight, but I can nurse," Louisa wrote prophetically.

On October 16, 1859, John Brown and a small group of supporters, including two of his sons, attacked and captured the federal arsenal at Harper's Ferry, Virginia. He expected his great slave revolution to break out and come to his aid. It didn't happen. Brown and his ragtag guerrillas managed to hang on to the arsenal for two days before it was retaken by federal troops. Brown's two sons were killed. He was tried and convicted of treason. On the second of December, John Brown was hanged.

"The execution of Saint John the Just," Louisa called it. All Concord turned out for the memorial meeting that same day. Emerson and Thoreau both spoke. The congregation sang a funeral dirge written by Frank Sanborn. It was Bronson Alcott who read the funeral service.

The weather was warm, a false spring, so warm that a rose bloomed in the garden. Louisa wrote a poem, "With a Rose, That Bloomed on the Day of John Brown's Martyrdom."

> No monument of quarried stone,
>   No eloquence of speech,
> Can grave the lessons on the land
>   His martyrdom will teach. . . .

The country was ripe for war.

FOURTEEN

"The Blood of the Mays Is Up!"

"JOHN BROWN MARTYRED & F. B. S. kidnapped," Louisa recorded in summing up the year 1859. "My first tale came out in the Atlantic & my pen began to pay."

Frank Sanborn had been arrested and charged with collaboration in the John Brown treason plot, but he was eventually freed. Louisa had gone from writing sentimental poems and stories about flowers, to romances, to stories that were darker and more thrilling. One of these, "Love and Self-Love," had brought her $50 from *Atlantic Monthly Magazine*.

Early in 1860 Louisa sat down to write a story that would show the evils of slavery. Remembering the brand she had seen on the face of runaway slave Anthony Burns, Louisa created a half-white slave branded with the initials *M.L.* It had a sinister plot involving abolition and an interracial love story, and it was too strong for the *Atlantic*. Louisa put it aside to submit elsewhere later and began writing "A Modern Cinderella," with Anna and John as hero and heroine. She was looking for plot material everywhere. Her "potboilers," as she called them, were enriching the Alcott Sinking Fund and had even bought a carpet for Orchard House.

The year 1860 was a calm before the storm of war. Frank Sanborn held a grand masquerade ball early in the year, for which Louisa made many of the costumes.

In March came the school festival that Bronson organized as superintendent of the Concord schools. Louisa wrote a song about Concord for it, and four hundred children sang her words. Bronson was in his element, staging a celebration similar to the old ones at the Temple School. He realized, as few educators did, that children needed recognition.

That spring Louisa and May went horseback riding— Louisa made them both riding habits—and Louisa acquired a "lover." He was handsome, he was Southern, he saw her on the railroad train and lost his heart at once. Louisa couldn't get rid of him and thought it all very funny.

In May Louisa's farce *Nat Batchelor's Pleasure Trip* was finally produced in Boston. But the main event of springtime was Anna's wedding, on May 23. It was Bronson and Abba's thirtieth anniversary. Anna was married in the Orchard House parlor, with the Alcott and Pratt families, the Emersons, Sanborn, Thoreau, and Elizabeth Peabody all there. Sam May, newly home from Europe, performed the ceremony. Anna wore silver-gray silk, with John's favorite lilies of the valley in her bodice and her hair. May, John's sister Carrie, and Louisa were her attendants. Louisa wore pepper-and-salt barege (a sheer openwork silk-and-wool fabric) and red flowers in her hair. After the ceremony there were cakes, and Concord grape wine, and some of last fall's cider from the keg in the Orchard House cellar. Under the elm tree on the lawn, the guests danced in pairs around the happy couple, and Mr. Emerson kissed the bride.

In late afternoon, after the newlyweds had left and the dishes had been washed, a procession of seventy schoolchildren came marching down the lane to serenade Bronson and Louisa with her Concord song. Bronson rushed to the cellar for apples to hand out, and led the children in Follow the Leader until they all were tired.

A few days later, John Brown's widow and her widowed daughter-in-law arrived in Concord and came to a sewing-circle meeting at Orchard House. Twenty ladies were expected, forty appeared, and by evening all of Concord's important men were there also. Louisa was greatly impressed by the sorrow and dignity of the Brown women.

There was a great deal of activity in Concord that summer. Harriet Tubman, the "woman called Moses" who had escaped from slavery herself and then returned to the South nineteen times to guide other runaways, was in town, for Concord was a major stop on the Underground Railway. The Hawthornes and their three children returned from England at the end of June. Young Julian Hawthorne promptly fell in love with May. At picnics and river trips, at swimming parties at Walden Pond, at his mother's Wednesday afternoon receptions and May's dancing class, he pursued her.

Louisa went swimming in her blue flannel bathing dress (with short skirt and pantaloons) and entered into the dancing and fun with enthusiasm. But as she wrote to her distant cousin Adeline May, May lived for "her crayons and dancing, father for his garden, mother for the world in general and I for my pens and ink."

All beginning authors have a "great book" in mind, a serious book that they hope will last long and will earn them

Nancy Hill-Joroff

ANNA BRONSON ALCOTT, C. 1860

Nancy Hill-Joroff

JOHN BRIDGE PRATT, C. 1860

the respect of the authors and mentors they themselves look up to. Louisa was no different. Her romances and thrillers, though she loved writing them, were turned out in a hurry for one reason only—money. She was in an intimidating situation most other beginners didn't face. She was the daughter of Bronson Alcott and Abba May; she had been raised on the greatest literature ever written; she had sat at the feet of the giants of her own time, such as Emerson. Now she wanted to write a "real novel."

She knew exactly what it would be about. Its title would be *Moods,* from a comment by Emerson that "Life is a train of moods like a string of beads; and as we pass through them they prove to be many-colored lenses, which paint the world in their own hue, and each shows us only what lies in its own focus."

She began in August. The book wrote itself in four weeks, during which she was caught up in the whirlwind of imagination that she called her "vortex" and rarely ate or slept. What she spun was the story of Ottila and Adam, a modern Samson and Delilah married on the impulse of passion, and of Sylvia, a sinner purified and redeemed by suffering. "Daresay nothing will come of it, but it *had* to be done, and I'm the richer for a new experience," Louisa summed up in her journal after she put the manuscript away to "settle."

One thing came of it almost at once. Emerson learned about *Moods* from Abba and offered to critique it.

That September Concord turned itself into a gymnasium where a Dr. Dio Lewis came to town and gave lectures, demonstrations, and gymnastics practice sessions. The sight of the Concord elders twisting themselves into contortions tickled Louisa's funnybone. She had good news that month also. The *Atlantic* published "A Modern Cinderella" and paid $75 for it. Louisa took time off to go to Boston and watch the review in honor of the visiting eighteen-year-old prince of Wales.

She did not go to Boston that winter. May did, to study art, until in December she was offered a post teaching drawing at Dr. Wilbur's Asylum in Syracuse, New York. Louisa sewed "like a steam-engine for a week" to get May's clothes ready. She was going to miss May terribly, and knew it; she was missing Anna, now snug in her own home and wrapped up in "dear John." But the John Brown Society asked her to write a poem to be read at the memorial meeting to be held in Boston on the first anniversary of Brown's execution. Louisa wrote the poem but didn't go, because she had no suitable gown. She wasn't proud of the poem, because she hadn't managed to say what she felt.

Christmas was quiet, with only Bronson, Abba, and Louisa at Orchard House. "[A]s Mother says, 'while there is a famine in Kansas we must n't ask for sugar-plums.' All the philosophy in our house is not in the study; a good deal is in the kitchen, where a fine old lady thinks high thoughts and does kind deeds while she cooks and scrubs."

Louisa recorded an income of $150 that year, all of it from writing.

In January of 1861, Louisa was still letting *Moods* "settle." She started another novel, tentatively called *Success*. Abba took sick, so Louisa corked up her inkstand to nurse her mother. Bronson held four Conversations at the Emerson house and made thirty dollars. Louisa suspected most of that had come anonymously from Emerson. One of the tales she had written for the *Atlantic* in 1859 was finally published— Louisa celebrated by treating herself to a new dress.

Louisa dug out the manuscript of *Moods* and spent the whole month of February "in a vortex," her brain racing so fast she could neither eat nor sleep. She shut herself into her bedroom, at the desk her mother had given her, wrapped in an old green-and-red party wrap that she called her "glory cloak," with the silk cap Abba had made for her perched on her head. At dusk she would emerge for a walk. Abba wandered in and out of the room, providing cups of tea. Bronson brought red apples and hard cider. Concord's winter social season was in full swing, but Louisa couldn't have cared less.

After three weeks of this Louisa was physically and mentally exhausted. Her head was spinning and her legs were shaking. She put aside the gold and ivory pen that had been a New Year's gift and took long walks and cold baths. She sent for Anna to come pull her out of her vortex with companionship and "frolic." Then she read the revised manuscript aloud to her assembled family, who sat up till midnight listening with wide eyes.

When she put down the manuscript, Louisa knew that even if it never came to anything, she had made her parents proud.

Abraham Lincoln, the rail-splitter from Illinois, was sworn in as the country's sixteenth president on March 4, 1861. Five and a half weeks later, the War Between the States began.

Seven southern states had seceded from the Union after Lincoln's election in the autumn of 1860. First of all had been South Carolina. Fort Sumter sat on an island in Charleston, South Carolina's harbor, and the Union troops had been ordered not to let it be taken. Lincoln was still hoping to avoid open conflict, but that was not to be. At 4:30 A.M. on Friday, April 12, Southern troops fired on Fort Sumter. The Union gunners within fired back.

It was a hopeless battle, but a gallant one. Smoke hung over Charleston harbor until early afternoon of April 13, when the officer in charge of Fort Sumter decided that surrender was his only choice.

It was now too late to save the Union without bloodshed. Bells of victory rang out in Charleston. Church bells rang out all over the divided country.

The Concord Artillery of the State Regiment, Massachusetts Voluntary Militia, was ordered to Washington, D.C., at once. They left Concord on Friday, April 19. Concord turned out in a mass to see them off, wearing red-white-and-blue cockades. Red, white, and blue were everywhere. Emerson's son Edward formed a company of Concord cadets that drilled for an hour and a half every dawn. All the women and girls of Concord began sewing for War Relief, and John Brown's daughters came to board at Orchard House.

"I've often longed to see war, and now I have my wish. I long to be a man; but as I can't fight, I will content myself with working for those who can," Louisa wrote. Stories were racing in her brain, but she had no time to write them.

The first summer of the war went on with little military action. Concord had its usual Fourth of July celebrations, a regatta, and fireworks after dark. May was back for the summer, teaching art at Frank Sanborn's school. Louisa sewed army shirts of Union blue, scraped lint out of sheeting for packing wounds, and wished she could do more. When the Willises invited her to join them in New Hampshire, she packed her best summer gowns (dandelion yellow and gray), her hat with green ribbons, her boots and notebooks, and took off for the Alpine House in Gorham.

Throughout the Union and the Confederacy, brand-new recruits, West Point graduates, and patriots on the home fronts waited eagerly for battle.

On Sunday, July 21, 1861, the confrontation came. It happened at a little town called Manassas Junction, only a carriage ride away from Washington, D.C. Manassas was on the main supply line for Richmond, the Confederate capital.

President Lincoln wanted the supply line cut before the Union volunteers' three-month enlistments ran out.

The Union troops were up at 2:00 A.M. getting into position. The Confederate troops were waiting. Early in the morning, the battle began. No one on either side was prepared for what was to follow. Both the Union and the Confederacy had expected the war to be over quickly. As rumors of battle spread, parties of spectators began driving out to watch—gentlemen with spyglasses, ladies in hoopskirts and straw picture hats, with their children and picnic baskets.

The battle was a disaster for both amateur armies. With the first blood, raw recruits panicked and ran, leaving their guns behind them. The spectators, Yankee and Rebel, panicked also. There was a rush for the only escape route, a narrow bridge across a small stream called Bull Run. A horse-drawn wagon tipped over on the bridge, blocking all passage. After that came chaos.

Bull Run was a Federal defeat, and a shock of harsh reality to both sides. Five Concord men were among the missing— dead or captured. One of them was Louisa's childhood friend Cyrus Hosmer.

After that Louisa was more determined than ever not to sit on the home front, quietly sewing like a proper lady.

For the moment, all she could do was help keep up morale, and write. Her stories grew darker. She sold two of them, "Whisper in the Dark" and "A Pair of Eyes," to publisher Frank Leslie, but he didn't publish them for another two years.

The Alcotts all gathered together at Orchard House for Abba's sixty-first birthday that autumn. Anna and John were very happy, and much as Louisa missed her sister, she was coming to love John like a brother. May continued teaching in Concord, and Elizabeth Peabody was asking Louisa to come to Boston and teach in her new "Kinder Garten." "Play & school 'jined,' " Louisa described it.

In January 1862, Louisa moved to Boston. Miss Peabody's school was in the Alcotts' former home at 20 Pinckney Street. She wanted Louisa to open another, on the other side of the Common. Louisa wasn't enthusiastic, but space was offered at the Warren Street Chapel, and she had learned to "take what comes," as she put it. The school did not bring in enough money to pay for Louisa's room and board, so she was forced to stay with relatives and friends.

It was humiliating to be in that position again. "Hate to visit people who ask me to help amuse others, and often longed for a crust in a garret with freedom and a pen. I never knew before what insolent things a hostess can do, nor what false positions poverty can push one into," she admitted in her journal. But she had promised to teach for six months, and she kept her word.

By April she was commuting back and forth to Concord every day. It was better than being beholden to others for her bed and board, and writing in her Orchard House bedroom was better than trying to write in someone else's home. Bronson and Abba understood her need to be left alone when the glory cloak was on and the red and green cap rampant on her head.

In May her six months of kindergarten teaching were over, and she was free. Louisa threw herself into writing thrilling tales for Frank Leslie. He wanted all she could produce, and he paid well. Henry Thoreau died that month, saddening all of Concord. He had been sick for some time.

All that summer and into the autumn, Louisa wrote her tales and letters. At Orchard House there was welcome news. Anna was going to make Bronson and Abba grandparents sometime in the spring. But the war news was bad.

"Anxious faces, beating hearts, and busy minds," Louisa wrote. "I like the stir in the air, and long for battle like a warhorse when he smells powder. The blood of the Mays is up!"

At Thanksgiving time she would be thirty years old. She was resolved not to sit on the sidelines any longer. A call had gone out for volunteers to nurse at army hospitals—not professionally trained nurses, for there was no such thing, but respectable women with some experience tending the sick. Louisa sent in her name.

On the eleventh of December she received a message telling her to report to the Union Hotel Hospital in Washington, D.C., where a Boston woman, Mrs. Hannah Ropes, was matron. Louisa packed her trunk with the black, brown, and gray dresses she had been told to bring, her brass inkstand and a copper teakettle, and the notes she had made from Florence Nightingale's *Notes on Nursing*. She set off for Boston that same day, in the December twilight, with May and Julian Hawthorne as her escorts.

All day on Friday, December 12, Louisa ran around Boston on last-minute errands, and at 5:00 P.M. she boarded the train for Washington, "full of hope and sorrow, courage and plans."

142

FIFTEEN

"The Air Is Bad Enough to Breed a Pestilence"

WASHINGTON, STILL AN UNFINISHED CITY of open sewers and mosquitoes, was settling down to the grim business of war. The Capitol building still lacked its dome. Soldiers, politicians, war profiteers, and escaping black slaves were everywhere. The hospital to which Louisa reported wasn't a hospital at all but a former hotel in Georgetown. It was near the river, an unhealthy area for anyone, let alone the wounded.

There was no regular military medical service when the Civil War broke out. There was no regular setup for any of the behind-the-lines services an army needed. After Fort Sumter, the War Department hurriedly established the United States Sanitary Commission. It was responsible for hospitals, relief work, and transport of the wounded. It was staffed by volunteers, funded by donations and fund-raisers.

Most of this work was done by women. The country's huge network of women's rights organizations, sewing circles, and charitable societies threw their money, labor, and managerial skills into war relief.

Clara Barton, founder of the American Red Cross, and Dorothea Dix, a pioneer in humane care of the insane, were in charge of choosing hospital nurses. The young, the romantic, and the irresponsible were weeded out. Those chosen provided their own aprons and dark dresses; their only "uniform" was a crocheted red headkerchief known as a rigolette. They received a bed in a hospital dormitory, meals, and $12 a month. For this they worked ceaselessly, with very few supplies, for at least twelve hours a day.

Louisa was shocked by conditions in the Union Hotel Hospital. She had studied Florence Nightingale's instructions for cleanliness and proper ventilation. Here windows were partly boarded up to protect the wards from looters who roamed the Washington streets. The air was either foul and suffocating, or damp and drafty. Walls were covered with worn wallpaper that could not be washed. Floors could not be scrubbed because they were covered with dust-catching carpet. There wasn't time to do much cleaning anyway.

Louisa was assigned an iron bed in a tiny room with two other nurses. It had one chair, one wardrobe, and a tin saucepan that the women used as a mirror when they brushed their hair. The fireplace was too small to burn anything but chips.

The hotel ballroom, divided up into wards, was not large enough to hold all the wounded. They spilled into corridors, reception areas, empty hotel bedrooms. Supposedly each nurse was to tend ten men, but usually she had to work with many more. When Louisa arrived, rumors of a coming battle at Fredericksburg, Virginia, were sweeping through the hospital, and any patients who could possibly be sent home or back to their regiments were being discharged. Their beds were needed.

Mrs. Ropes, the matron in charge, hurriedly told Louisa her duties. Among other things, she was to empty bedpans as soon as they'd been used and change the patients' underclothes at least once a week. Escaped slaves did the wash and ran errands. Any patients well enough to walk acted as orderlies.

On that first day "on the floor," Louisa took care of a man dying from a shot through the lungs, nursed pneumonia patients, and witnessed at least one death. And that was only the beginning.

Louisa recorded the routine in her journal. "Up at six, dress by gaslight, run through my ward & fling up the windows though the men grumble & shiver; but the air is bad enough to breed a pestilence . . . cold, damp, dirty, full of vile odors from the wounds, kitchens, wash rooms, & stables."

On and on the list went: breakfast of "fried beef, salt butter, husky bread & washy coffee"; see that the patients' faces and hands were washed with strong brown soap; dish out rations for her wards; supervise bed making and floor sweeping. Change the dressings on minor wounds herself. Help the doctor attend to more serious ones. Fetch the medicines needed for her patients. Rush around in search of pillows, sheets, and blankets. In the afternoon, while the patients rested, read aloud or write letters for those men who wanted it.

Some simply needed someone to sit by them and help them die. Louisa had kept deathwatch with Elizabeth, but that had been nothing like this.

The operations were the worst, especially the amputations, so often needed because of shattered bones or gangrene. A nurse had to pick the bone fragments out of the wound stump before it could be bandaged. A nurse had to break the news of the amputation afterward when the patient returned to consciousness—if there had been enough anesthesia to *make* him unconscious. Often there wasn't.

At dawn on December 16 the wounded from the Battle of Fredericksburg began to arrive, wave on wave of them. One of the doctors came rushing in to tell of ambulances clogging streets on which still more wounded lay.

Forty-five of them were sent to Union Hotel Hospital. Some of them became part of Louisa's memories forever. There was Robert Bane from Michigan, just the kind of jolly teenage boy she liked best. He had lost an arm and was eager to get an artificial one and plunge back into battle. Richard Fitzgerald was a cavalryman with an Irish brogue. Louisa thought of her own "boys," Llewellyn Willis and Alf Whitman and all the rest, and she was cold with fear.

Above all, there was a gentle blacksmith from Virginia named John Suhre, who had taken a Confederate bullet in his left lung. Night after night he lay there, struggling for breath and waiting for death to come. Night after night Louisa sat with him, with her small blue-banded water jug, the dim lamplight shining on her chestnut hair. She listened as he whispered slowly about his sister and his widowed mother. She wrote the letter he dictated painfully, a letter to his brother. They both knew the brother's answer would not come in time.

Christmas was coming. Evergreens garlanded the hospital wards and wreaths hung in the halls. Louisa received a kind of Christmas present—a letter from Frank Leslie's publications announcing that Miss Alcott's story, "Pauline's Passion and Punishment," had won the story contest's hundred-dollar prize. Louisa took night duty, making the rounds of the wards on the midnight-to-noon shift, "when sleep & death have the house to themselves."

Now that she was on night duty, Louisa stole time from her sleep to explore the wartime city. She was so weary, and her brain raced so, that she could not sleep anyway. She saw the marching infantry, the lines of army wagons, the gold lace on officers' blue uniforms. The Federal mansions and neat row houses like those in Boston. The unfinished Capitol. The shacks of Washington's free blacks, and the huts of runaway slaves. Capitol Hill was desolate. A cross-section of America's population jostled and crowded on the streets of America's capital city.

Sergeant Bane went home to Michigan. John the blacksmith died. Others took their place, in a never-ending chain.

On New Year's Day all the bells of the city rang, and the Emancipation Proclamation was announced. To the abolitionists, it was about time.

January was raw and cloudy. Louisa continued her exploration of the city and her night duty in the wards. She developed a racking cough like that she'd had at Fruitlands. But she kept on. She could not afford to give in to sickness. Disease was sweeping through the wards—measles and chicken pox and scarlet fever; typhus and pneumonia. Mrs. Ropes, the matron, was felled with typhus, and rumor spread that she was dying.

Louisa's cough grew worse. She called it a winter cold and kept on going. She felt icy cold. Everything blurred before her eyes, and she told herself it was from lack of sleep. Then she came down with fever.

Her face, when she looked at her reflection in the tin saucepan, was a death mask. Dr. Stipp, the surgeon in charge,

LOUISA MAY ALCOTT, SOMETIME IN THE 1860s

ordered her to her bed. She crawled in, unsure whether she was hot or freezing.

Night and day were as one. Vaguely she saw faces bending over her. She swallowed, obediently, the massive doses of calomel Dr. Stipp prescribed. Calomel was mercurous chloride, a very strong laxative used to purge the system of poisons. Because of the pestilent conditions in the war hospitals, doctors were prescribing calomel in large quantities in the forlorn hope it would ward off pneumonia, consumption, and inevitable death.

Delirium possessed her. Visions of forceps and sponges and other hospital apparatus came and went. She thought she heard an organ grinder playing, and an army chaplain preaching. The doctors, and Dorothea Dix, came and went, and she did not know them. Mrs. Ropes died. Louisa, her mouth dry and her tongue thick with fever, tossed and turned weakly, muttered and slept, and woke in terror.

She came up out of the web of dreams one January day to find a familiar silver-haired figure stooping over her. Father, of all people . . . searching her face with the same fearful, helpless look in his blue eyes that she had seen there when Elizabeth lay dying . . .

Louisa sank back into sleep.

Bronson nursed her until she was well enough to be moved. On January 21, 1863, Dorothea Dix packed a basket of medicine and wine, tea and cologne, a blanket and pillow and New Testament. Louisa's "boys," those who were well enough to stir from the hospital, went to the railroad station to see her off. She was scarcely conscious enough to notice.

Louisa had been at the hospital exactly forty days, and she was now herself a casualty of war.

SIXTEEN

"For a Fortnight I Hardly Ate, Slept or Stirred"

LOUISA'S NIGHT AND DAY on the railroad cars passed in a nightmare. She drifted in and out of consciousness, aware only that her father was there and that she was going home. At last they reached Boston. Bronson had hoped to go straight on to Concord, but Louisa was far too sick. They spent the night with the Thomas Sewalls at 98 Chestnut Street. In the middle of the night Louisa was seized with a fit so alarming that a doctor had to be called.

By morning she was somewhat better, and at 4:00 P.M. father and daughter started out again. Glimpses of reality penetrated into Louisa's fevered brain. Una Hawthorne, Nathaniel's daughter, suddenly appearing on the Concord train; cradling Louisa in her arms for the rest of the jolting journey, Louisa's head resting on her shoulder. May at the train depot, her face shocked. Orchard House looming darkly behind winter-stark trees. And then her mother, bewildered, frightened.

Somehow they got Louisa up Orchard House's steep stairs. She was in her own room, with May's owl gazing into space from the chimneypiece. The winter clothes, the hoops, the corset were being stripped off her. She was in her own bed, staring upward into what she was convinced was a roofless sky.

It was months before she was able to leave her room again.

For weeks typhoid raged through Louisa's weary body. Strange dreams—out of her unconsciousness, out of her hospital memories—haunted her. She thought she was in a twilight heaven. She thought she was being burned as a witch. She thought she was being tempted to worship the devil. She thought she was nursing millions of sick men who never died and never got well.

The worst dream, the ongoing one, was that she was married to a terrifying, handsome Spaniard with very soft hands. He was all in black velvet, always saying "Lie still, my dear." Out of the mists, out of closets, through windows, and all night long he came, until Louisa cried out in something she thought was Latin, an appeal to the Pope for aid. Afterward, remembering, Louisa concluded the ever-present stranger with the Mediterranean face had probably been her mother.

After three weeks of delirium Louisa came back to consciousness to learn that she had nearly died and was still terribly sick. She looked in the mirror and a stranger looked back at her, gaunt and hollow-eyed, all the knee-length chestnut hair of which she had been so proud cut off. Now she, like Elizabeth in her last illness, had to wear caps to cover her shorn head.

When she forced herself to stand her legs collapsed under her. Her mouth was full of sores. Every part of her ached.

She couldn't eat. She couldn't sleep for more than brief periods. She couldn't breathe. Worst of all, her mind wouldn't work right. She couldn't remember things. She had delusions. It was as though she had slipped, frighteningly, into one of her own thrilling tales of strange drugs, hallucinations, and mind control.

Her father and mother rarely left her side. The doctor came daily. May sang to her and read to her. Letters and gifts poured in. Lu Willis had died the previous year, but Hamilton came, and Cousin Lizzie Wells, and Anna, who was close to giving birth.

Louisa's pay from the Sanitary Commission came—$10. That, lasting sickness, and a web of dreams were what she received for serving her country, but she did not regret it.

She tried to get used to her "new body," but the body and mind wouldn't cooperate. She had to learn all over again how to read and write and sew. By March she was able to sit up nearly all day and to eat more normally. She dusted her books and sorted out her "piece bag" of fabric remnants. She read and read. "[T]yphus," Louisa wrote, "was not inspiring."

On March 22 she left her room at last.

Six nights later Bronson came home from Boston beaming with joy. Though worn out with caring for Louisa, he had begun two series of Conversations that season. That particular night his weariness was forgotten, for Anna's child had been born. It was not the "Louisa Caroline" they had been expecting, but a fine boy.

"*Where* is my *niece?*" Louisa demanded by mail to Anna two days later. "I wish you could have seen the performances on Sat. eve. We were sitting deep in a novel & had given up expecting father owing to the snow, when the door burst open & in he came all wet & white, waving his bag & calling out, 'Good news!' . . . [W]e three opened our mouths &

screamed for about two minutes; then mother began to cry, I to laugh, & May to pour out questions. . . . Father had told every one he met from Emerson to the coach driver."

John and Anna named their son Frederick Alcott Pratt. Abba promptly went to visit her first grandchild, and Louisa began sewing baby clothes for her new nephew. As New England spring began to bloom, she was able to take walks and carriage drives. Everything seemed so new and beautiful that she felt born again. "To go very near to death teaches one to value life," she wrote soberly.

Now that she was able to function again, however slowly, Louisa sized up the family situation and found, as usual, a need for money. She had not earned any for months, and she, not Bronson, was now the family's main support. Her friend Frank Sanborn had become editor of the *Boston Commonwealth*, and he suggested she edit for publication the letters she'd written home from the hospital. Louisa produced three "Hospital Sketches," altering names and leaving out scandalous bits such as the lady volunteer who made a habit of persuading dying soldiers to make out wills in her favor. The war was still raging, and Louisa was too patriotic to do anything that would damage home-front support.

To Louisa's surprise, the "Sketches" were an immediate and enormous success. The hundred-dollar prize from Frank Leslie arrived, which also eased her mind. As her strength returned, Louisa threw herself into writing and house repairs. With Abba still off being a grandma, May and Louisa gave Orchard House a thorough going-over. May painted woodwork and put up wallpaper in the parlors. Louisa's Alcott Sinking Fund (her name for her savings) provided the wallpaper, new carpet and a rug, plus the proper "suite of furniture" for her own room that she had long dreamed of.

Spurred by the success of "Hospital Sketches," Louisa dug

out her manuscript of *Moods*. Publishers were now seeking her out, rather than the other way around, and she planned to make the most of the situation. *Two* publishers wanted book rights to "Hospital Sketches." One was Roberts Brothers, whose editor had told her to stick to her teaching because she couldn't write. The other was Redpath, which was known to be abolitionist. Louisa had no trouble choosing Redpath, especially since she liked the contract terms.

With "Hospital Sketches" Louisa had gone from being anonymous (using no author name) to pseudonymous (using a made-up author name), but by the time the book edition of the "Sketches" was published, the whole Boston area knew that "Tribulation Periwinkle" was really Bronson Alcott's daughter.

In the first week of July, news of the bloody Battle of Gettysburg burst upon the country. The three-day battle marked the turning point of the Civil War, and the Concord troops were a part of it. Louisa had arranged that some of Redpath's profits from "Hospital Sketches" should go to a fund that had been started for war orphans. Still gaunt and weak from her illness, she remained in Concord that summer, regaining her strength—and writing. In addition to the stories, there were many letters to and from publishers, friends, and her "boys" from the hospital.

In September the Concord troops that had fought at Gettysburg came home. All over Concord flags fluttered in the breeze, and wreaths and WELCOME HOME banners were everywhere. Louisa interrupted her writing to put on one of her "hospital dresses" and tied her nurse's red rigolette over her hair.

A drum corps of eight little boys beat its heart out and fifes played a martial air. The Lexington Road was lined with cheering spectators as the little column of soldiers came into

CONCORD IN THE 1860s

view, marching in parade formation toward Concord center. Suddenly the captain spotted the tall, tired figure in plain dark dress and army-nurse headdress, and whipped his sword from its scabbard. His command rang out. Sixty pairs of feet stopped marching. Sixty citizen-soldiers came to attention, facing Orchard House. Sixty rifle butts rapped smartly against the ground. The veterans of Gettysburg were honoring Louisa May Alcott as one of their own.

Bronson's mother died that autumn, and Anna and little Freddy paid a long visit to Orchard House. Redpath asked Louisa to edit one of their many small papers, but she was afraid to try that yet and refused. She worked away on revisions of *Moods,* longing to have it published, but she was afraid to submit it to a publisher. This was her "real book," and she was protective of it. She was thinking of going to Port Royal, South Carolina, to teach the escaped slaves who had formed a colony there. Louisa had to give that up, but she spent a lot of time and effort on the great fund-raising Sanitary Commission Fair to be held in Boston in December. She dramatized six "Scenes from Dickens," and acted in them as well. The six performances raised $2,500 for the fair.

As 1863 ended Louisa found she had earned nearly six hundred dollars from her writing alone in the year, during nearly half of which she had been far from well. She had spent less than a hundred dollars on herself, but she had put a new roof on Orchard House, supported her family, and given $70 to May. She was now an established writer. Frank Sanborn had told her that any publisher would be glad to get a book from her, and both Roberts and Redpath were actively seeking one.

Anna was quite sick during the early part of 1864, and Abba went to look after her, so Louisa was once again housekeeper at Orchard House. She put writing aside. She was finding, anyway, that a steady grind of story production could make even the most fertile imagination run dry at times.

During this time, Louisa began letting editors get a look at *Moods*. They all liked it but found things wrong, particularly the length. Louisa refused to cut. She turned out more dark thrillers for Frank Leslie and began publishing under the pseudonym "A. M. Barnard." She wrote a fervent antislavery story called "An Hour," but was not surprised when it was rejected as too "political." It was later published in the Boston *Commonwealth*.

The war was still going on. A cousin was killed in the Battle of the Wilderness. Nathaniel Hawthorne went on a walking trip in New Hampshire with his friend, former president Franklin Pierce, and was found dead while on it. Louisa at last broke away from work and home duties for two weeks at Gloucester with May, and it did both her body and her imagination good. "[A] jolly time boating, driving, charading dancing & picnicing. One mild moonlight night a party of us camped out on Norman's Woe . . . lying on the rocks singing, talking, sleeping & rioting up & down. We had a fine time & took coffee at all hours."

That autumn Louisa was working away on another book (*Success,* retitled *Work,* based on her own experiences) when she was suddenly possessed by an idea of how to reorganize *Moods* in a way that would make it considerably shorter. She dug it out of its spidery cupboard and plunged into her whirlwind. "The fit was on strong & for a fortnight I hardly ate slept or stirred but wrote, wrote like a thinking machine in full operation. When it was all rewritten, without copying, I found it much improved though I'd taken out ten chapters & sacrificed many of my favorite things."

The manuscript was sold at once, though Louisa found it

hard to believe her favorite work would ever see the light. She gave a manuscript copy to her mother for Abba's sixty-fourth birthday. Abba had not been well. For a week Orchard House became a hospital as first Anna, then Freddy, then Abba, then John Pratt, and then Louisa all lay sick there.

Moods was rushed into galley proofs. Louisa, reading them, had the sensation of reading someone else's story, and it was not a good one. She wrote Christmas stories at publishers' demand and sold Frank Sanborn her antislavery story. And she kept on with her war work, sewing towels and bed sacks for Massachusetts' black army unit.

On Christmas Day, *Moods* was published. Louisa received her ten author copies on Christmas Eve. She had no idea what was about to happen.

"For a week wherever I went I saw, heard & talked 'Moods;' found people laughing or crying over it, & was continually told . . . how fine a thing I'd done. I was glad but not proud, I think, for it has always seemed as if 'Moods' grew in spite of me, & that I had little to do with it except to put into words the thoughts that would not let me rest until I had."

By New Year's Day, 1865, the first edition was sold out and another was being printed. Booksellers were selling copies by the hundreds. "Tribulation Periwinkle" had her public success at last.

When the reviews came in Louisa found that many critics did not understand at all the ideas she had so wanted to put forward, partly because of all that cutting. But the book was a success. Louisa began receiving fan letters, many of which tickled her funnybone. Frank Leslie asked Louisa to be a regular contributor to a new paper of his. Louisa, capitalizing on her new fame, demanded payment in advance—$50—

and got it. She had graduated into the ranks of writers who write only what they have presold.

April came, a time of lilacs in New England. On April 2 and 3, the Confederate capital at Richmond fell to Union troops. On April 9, 1865, the long war ended quietly with Lee's surrender to Grant at Appomattox Court House, Virginia. Louisa went to Boston to be part of the celebrations.

On Friday, April 14, exactly four years after Fort Sumter fell, President Lincoln and his wife attended a performance of *Our American Cousin* at Ford's Theatre in Washington to celebrate the end of the war. John Wilkes Booth, a Southern sympathizer and brother of the actor Edwin Booth whom Louisa so admired, shot the president to death.

The news reached Boston the next day and the city went into mourning. The sudden change from celebration to sorrow, the wave of emotion that bonded strangers together, was something Louisa never forgot.

Anna's second son, John Sewall Pratt, was born in June. *Moods* and Louisa's thrillers were bringing in money, and the family was fairly comfortable, so Louisa began dreaming an old dream. She wanted to see Europe; she wanted to make the Grand Tour as Mr. Emerson and so many great writers had done. The dream was rekindled in July when a relative inquired whether Louisa would consider going abroad as a companion to her sister. The invitation was withdrawn because Louisa spoke no French or German, but it had put an idea into Louisa's mind. Many ladies traveled expense-free as companions; why couldn't she?

An opportunity soon arose. Anna Weld, the invalid daughter of a Boston shipping merchant, wanted to go abroad with her half-brother and needed a genteel woman, experienced in nursing, to go with her. Would Miss Alcott be interested?

Miss Alcott would.

They sailed from Boston on the *China* on the nineteenth of July. Louisa could scarcely believe her dream was coming true, and in many ways it wasn't. She felt a sudden wave of apprehension and homesickness as they sailed out of the harbor.

As it turned out, she was not a very good sailor. And in spite of—or perhaps because of—her own recent serious illness and the suffering she had witnessed in the army hospital, she did not have much patience with Anna Weld's aches and pains.

The real problem, aside from the difficulty of bending her independent spirit, after a period of self-employment, to an employer's whims, was the itinerary. Louisa longed for the excitements of Europe's beautiful cities. Anna Weld wanted quiet places to rest. Liverpool was dirty, London was drizzly, and Anna was ill. Louisa managed to go about quietly in the rain, seeing Westminster Abbey and feeling as though she'd stepped into a novel. She hated the English weather.

She was seasick all the way across the English Channel. The little party moved from Ostende to Brussels, Belgium, where Louisa wished they could stay a month instead of just two days. From there to Cologne, Germany . . . to a voyage up the Rhine . . . to a small spa town where they lingered for a month. Letters from home—the first in two months—lifted Louisa's spirits. They drifted from one German city to another. Then on to Lausanne, Switzerland, and to Vevey, a resort town on Lake Lucerne popular with English visitors. Anna's brother settled his sister and Louisa into a quiet *pension,* and he left for Paris. Louisa wished she could go there, too.

She went "owling about," taking the sights and sounds in wherever she could. She stored away memories of the people she saw. In November, Ladislas Wisniewski arrived at the pension. He was twenty years old and had fled his native Poland after the insurrection he had been part of failed. Ladislas was fun-loving and agreeable, he had had a romantic past, he played music beautifully, and he wanted to learn English. Louisa and Anna Weld gave him English lessons, and he taught them French.

With Ladislas there, life in Vevey became much more interesting to both Anna Weld and Louisa. He was some years younger than Louisa, and he promptly became one of her "boys." What romance existed was probably between him and Anna Weld, who was a wealthy heiress. But Louisa loved his personality and company, and they had long walks and talks and sails on the lake together.

In December Louisa and Anna Weld said farewell to a disconsolate Ladislas and joined George Weld in Geneva, Switzerland. From there they went on to the French Riviera. George left his sister and her companion at a pension in Nice and hurried back to America.

For Louisa, the winter was full of dull days and homesickness. Anna Weld was pining for Ladislas, and he for her, and both were using Louisa as confidante. There was a New Year's Eve ball at the pension, but the two Americans felt uncomfortable and lonely. In February they took an apartment of their own, with a respectable old French governess as landlady and chaperone. Louisa was already thinking of going home.

She decided to leave in May. On the first of that month Louisa boarded a train for Paris, feeling like a bird that had finally been freed. Now, at last, she could see some of Europe in her own style! The money from her writing had provided her that freedom.

Ladislas joined Louisa in Paris and they had two delicious weeks seeing the sights. From there Louisa went to England, staying with friends near London in an old thatched-roof farmhouse. Now she was no longer lonely, for friends of friends from the publishing and Boston intellectual worlds scooped her up. She saw all the historic and literary sights and received royalties for an English publication of *Moods*.

In July she sailed for home. Two weeks of sick, stormy days, and then Louisa saw her brother-in-law's friendly face waiting for her on the Boston wharf.

She reached home on July 20, 1866, a year and a day after she had sailed away. After the first excitement, Louisa found many changes. Bronson was placid, but Abba looked sick and old. Anna was not very well. The two Pratt boys had grown like weeds and were more appealing to "Auntie Wee" than ever.

Louisa threw herself at once into writing. The family, as usual, needed money. Publishers were clamoring for stories, and they were paying well. Louisa wasn't rich by any means, but she knew she was on the brink of feeling secure. What was even better, Cousin Samuel Sewall, a lawyer and women's rights activist, was willing to handle her money and make investments for her.

Louisa wrote a long story, "A Modern Mephistopheles," working at night after the family was in bed. Abba was ill and needed nursing, so Louisa got a hired girl in to do the housework. The story was rejected as too sensational. Louisa put it away for future use and fell to work again. Frank Leslie contracted with her for a story a month at $50 each; Louisa agreed, hoping she could fulfill the deadlines. Through the fall and into winter, Abba and Anna were still ill. "Very hard times all around," Louisa told her journal.

By November Abba was on the mend, but Louisa was forced to admit, "I never expect to see the strong, energetic 'Marmee' of old times." All her mother's abundant chestnut hair was gone. From now on, Abba would be a shriveled old lady with thin white hair and a cap, bowed down with age.

The Pratts went to board in East Boston for the winter. Louisa was sorry, yet relieved; she needed quiet. Bronson left on a lecture trip in the West. One more care removed, temporarily, from Louisa's shoulders. He came back a few days before Christmas, "thin, tired, hungry & dirty, very glad to get home to his cider & berries & be cuddled by his old lady." He was showing the effects of wear and age.

So was Louisa. By December she was feeling sick almost all the time. She had heavy colds, and was aching with rheumatism. The dampness of the Union Hotel Hospital had continued the harm done by the chills at Fruitlands years before. Louisa knew that she had never been "right" since the hospital, perhaps would never be "right." She could no longer count on energy, or endless imagination, to produce stories in spite of anything. Now that they were in demand, she was always conscious that she might not finish them on time, might not be able to fight off headaches, coughs, and chills. All the same, she had written twelve tales in less than three months, along with her other responsibilities. That wasn't bad. Neither was the nearly $1,200 she had earned from royalties and from the writing she had done since coming home.

January of 1867 brought more of the same. Louisa's journal entries grew terse. For a month she did nothing but sit in the dark and ache. In February Abba suffered from a bout of rheumatic fever and had to have an operation on her eyes for iritis, a painful inflammation related to rheumatism. By May Louisa was recording, "Still gaining, but all feeble. Mother half blind, Father lame & I weak, nervous & used up generally."

Slowly the tide began to turn as warm weather came. Uncle Sam May gave Louisa and May money to go to Clark's

Island, off the coast of Massachusetts, for vacation. Many friends were there, including Frank Sanborn, and the break did Louisa good.

She came home to find bills accumulating. "I dread debt more than the devil!" she wrote emphatically in her journal.

In September she was able to stop worrying. Horace Fuller, publisher of *Merry's Museum*, asked Louisa to become the magazine's editor. She would be expected to read manuscripts, and to write one story and one editorial a month, and would be paid $500 a year. Louisa said she'd try.

Thomas Niles, by now a partner in Roberts Brothers, also came to Louisa with an idea. He needed a nice book for girls and thought that she could write it. Louisa wasn't enthusiastic. If she was going to write for young readers again—and a book-length project, not a group of stories—she would prefer to write for boys. She *knew* boys, she pointed out. But Thomas Niles wanted a book for girls.

In the end, Louisa said she'd try.

SEVENTEEN

Little Women

IF LOUISA WERE GOING to fill all these professional obliga-
tions, she knew she had to live alone—in Boston. Fortunately, thanks to the salary guaranteed her as an editor, she
could. This time she took lodging not on Beacon Hill, but at
6 Hayward Place, just off Washington Street, where Boston's
successful publishers had offices.

Louisa was living the ideal writer's life: a combination of
city and country, privacy and family. But now, instead of
being a beginner trying to sell stories and looking for short-
term jobs to pay the rent, she was a career woman with an
established reputation. On October 28, 1867, she moved to
Boston with her own furniture, feeling as though she were
going camping in a new country.

She promptly named her one-room apartment "Gamp's

Garret," in honor of the immortal Sairy Gamp, a comic Dickens character she had often played in theatricals, and announced she would be "at home" with "cowcumber sandwiches" to all comers. Socially and professionally, Louisa found life in Boston lively. The Radical Club, to which Bronson and Emerson both belonged, was in full swing, and she and her father went together. She gave her program of Dickens monologues, *Mrs. Jarley's Waxworks,* for charity several times. The theater and opera season sparkled for Louisa. Charles Dickens appeared, on one of his American reading and lecture tours. Louisa went to hear him and was as disappointed as she had been a year earlier in London. Why, she wondered, did a man of his age and stature have to skip onto the stage with a diamond ring on each hand, "two rivers of watch guard" across his middle, and his thin gray hair curled, looking and sounding like a worn-out actor? She was disillusioned with the man, but never with his writing.

In November, May joined Louisa on Hayward Place, commuting daily between there and Concord. May was teaching several drawing classes and expected to be earning $50 a month. "Our Raphael," Louisa called her.

Louisa's work was going well, though she didn't enjoy writing editorials. In 1867 she had reached her goal of earning $1,000 a year. The year 1868 promised even more, for besides her editorial work she had agreed to write two short stories a month for *The Youth's Companion,* and Frank Leslie wanted all the stories she would send him—preferably one or two a month, at $50 to $100 each. Other publishers were eager for whatever pieces of writing she could spare them. She was setting herself a hard winter's work. But, after all, she had written twenty-five stories in 1867, plus a volume of twelve fairy tales, the currently popular literature form for children.

And then there was faithful editor Thomas Niles, who wanted a book about real girls, for girls.

The hyacinths bloomed in her window garden in January 1868, and Louisa took it as a good omen. The *New York Ledger* was running a series of columns of advice to young women, each written by a noted personality, and begged Louisa to contribute. She wrote an article titled "Happy Women." It was about "old maids. . . . I put in my list all the busy, useful, independent spinsters I know, for liberty is a better husband than love to many of us." She felt like a "happy millionaire."

In between writing, theater going, and play acting, Louisa carried on her loving family tasks. She made a bonnet for May, a flannel wrapper for Abba, costumes for the plays. She stayed with Anna and Johnny while John Pratt and Freddie were visiting in Concord. Anna's hearing had failed, and two-year-old Johnny could only talk to his "Marmar" through her ear trumpet.

By the first of March Louisa was needed back in Concord. She hated leaving her quiet room, but she could look with pride on having written ten short stories and eight long ones, read and edited many manuscripts, and performed for charity twelve times since the first of the year. Nine of those performances had been in the past week, despite her being hoarse with a heavy cold. And back at Orchard House, Marmee had the sunny room, the many comforts, Louisa had always wanted to provide for her. More and more, she was referring to her mother by the old babyhood name. And more and more, Abba was becoming, as she was soon to refer to herself, an "old baby."

Louisa didn't get around to tackling Mr. Niles's book project until late spring. By then, Bronson himself was talking to Thomas Niles about possible publication of his own "great work," *Tablets*, and bringing up the subject of a fairy-tale book by Louisa. No, he wanted a *girls'* story, Mr. Niles stressed again.

In May, Louisa began writing. She had no idea how to begin, for the kind of book Niles had in mind had never been written before. Girls of Louisa's generation wept over books like *The Wide, Wide World,* a tear-jerker about a delicate orphan who, after many sufferings, becomes a pure, good woman and is rewarded with a storybook happy ending. Louisa and Anna had wept over *The Wide, Wide World* also, but their real reading had been in their parents' books. What Niles was after was something different from either, an account of life as lived by typical American girls in a typical American family.

Louisa had not lived such a typical life, but she did understand what *family* meant. She hadn't known many girls, but she did know her sisters. She had used Anna, May, and Elizabeth as characters in short stories, and she had always thought of writing an adult book about her "Pathetic Family."

In her bedroom at Orchard House in May 1868, while Bronson's gardens bloomed outside her windows, Louisa set to work.

"Christmas won't be Christmas without any presents," grumbled Jo, lying on the rug.

"It's so dreadful to be poor!" sighed Meg, looking down at her old dress.

"I don't think it's fair for some girls to have plenty of pretty things, and other girls nothing at all," added little Amy, with an injured sniff.

"We've got Father and Mother and each other," said Beth contentedly from her corner.

In four short sentences—from instinct, editorial experience, or her dramatic skills—Louisa introduced the four sisters and made them come alive. Anna became Meg, the pretty one, the proper one, the "little mother" who could remember the "good days." Elizabeth was Beth, the quiet homebody, "Little Tranquility," the family conscience. May, the letters of her name transposed, became Amy, the artistic one who reached for elegance and usually got her own way. And Louisa herself—a tall, thin stringbean, proud of the chestnut hair that was her one beauty, given to moods and stubbornness and blunt speaking—became indelibly, immortally, Jo March, who wished she were a boy and meant to be a writer. March was a fittingly storm-tossed pseudonym for May.

Louisa was writing, very definitely, a book about Mays, with all the family temperament and heritage. The guiding spirit of the four March girls was Marmee: Abba, with all the rough edges and fits of anger lovingly removed. Yet even those were present between the lines. Marmee was Abba in her later, mellow years, not the turbulent ones of Fruitlands and before.

Louisa didn't write Bronson into her book at all. She may have decided he was too unusual to be believed in a book for young readers. She *knew* his ideas were too controversial. And she remembered that in her childhood, much as she had loved her father, the happiest times had been when he wasn't there. Mr. March was an offstage presence, a chaplain off in the Civil War as Louisa had gone off to the war.

By now Louisa was such an experienced writer that she had learned exactly how she worked best. Not for her was the careful outlining of plots and themes, the writing and rewriting. She knew, as Bronson had found out, that for people like them too much polishing could take the life out of the story. Louisa's most successful stories had come out of the well of

169

her unconscious, when she was swept along for hours "in a vortex." What criticism *Moods* had received had been because of things left out in the cutting and editing she had reluctantly agreed to.

Louisa did have a minimal skeleton for her book: *Pilgrim's Progress*. It would be the story of four girls on such a pilgrimage, with their burdens of character flaws and disappointments, through the Valley of Humiliation, the Slough of Despond, the temptations of Vanity Fair. But the Celestial City would be not the kind of New Eden Bronson had dreamed of for Fruitlands, but the kind of secure, loving extended family life Louisa was a part of, and the development of the sisters' gifts and talents for the good of others and their own fulfillment as wise women.

The town was Concord—as it had been in Louisa's girlhood and still was. Louisa was writing about the Hillside days, but the March home sounds more like Orchard House, with the wide archway between living and dining rooms that became a natural frame for plays. Of course there were plays in the book—written by Jo (who acted all the men's parts, with sword and boots), with pretty Meg letting down her inhibitions as romantic heroines. The costumes, and many of the girls' own clothes, came out of rag bags and donations from rich relatives, just as the Alcotts' own clothes had for so long.

The other characters came easily, for Louisa had spent a lifetime making mental and written notes. Through all the hard times, she had, like Dickens, never lost the ability to see the comic side. So into the book went the May relations, the kind ones and the condescending ones. In went the townspeople of Concord and Still River. In went the editors who had helped her and the ones who had patronized her. In went John Pratt, renamed Brooke for his family's connection with the Brook Farm communal experiment. The romance of John and Anna would provide the book's love story, for Louisa was professional enough to realize one was needed, and she refused to make it revolve around Jo.

She needed a contrast between rich and poor, to show that while the Marches were poor in material things they were still blessed with more than many others. Onto the stage of her story paraded Aunt March, old, bossy, aristocratic, constantly reminding Marmee that she had married beneath her, but under the crustiness, begrudgingly kind. There was more than a trace of the legendary Aunt Dorothy Quincy Hancock, as she was in old age, in Aunt March. For kindly Aunt Carroll, and the Marches' other well-to-do friends, Louisa had a host of relatives on which to draw. The poorest characters, such as the Hummels, came directly from Abba's experiences as a social worker in the Boston slums.

Next to shabby Hillside, in the way such things happened in old New England towns, Louisa planted a mansion similar to Grandfather May's. She put Grandfather May, with his wisdom and kindness and autocratic ways, in as Mr. Lawrence, to whom she gave a touch of Emerson as well. And for the boy in the story, she invented "the Lawrence boy."

Laurie Lawrence—born Theodore, a name he despised because his schoolmates called him Dora—was a boy after Louisa's own heart. She made him up out of memories of Ladislas, and Alf Whitman. Laurie, at the time of his first appearance, was alone and lonely and recovering from illness, just as Ladislas had been. He loved music, just as Ladislas did. He was "all boy," but he had a sensitive, artistic side. He accepted Jo's boyishness, built up her belief in herself, and gave her the courage to let her tender side show. It was a wonder Louisa didn't let Jo fall in love with him—but she didn't. It was no wonder at all that he fell in love with Jo.

Through the month of May and into June Louisa's pen raced over the blue-lined sheets of paper. Everyone loved a holiday story, so she started hers at Christmas—one of those Christmases she knew so well, "without any presents." There was one of Louisa's thrilling melodramas (with Jo as author and swashbuckling hero), and the Puritan lesson of self-sacrifice, when the March girls gave away their breakfast—shades of that "dear plummy cake" back at the Temple School! From there on the story spun itself out with each girl in turn being the main character in a chapter. The incidents came straight out of Louisa's memory and her journal. There was even a Pickwick Club, and a *Pickwick Portfolio* (like Alcott family newspapers, *The Olive Leaf* and *The Pickwick*), and a private post office like the one Abba had created out at Fruitlands. And there were all the wonderful outdoor activities and festivals that were part of Concord winters and summertimes.

By the end of June Louisa had written twelve chapters. Mr. Niles wanted twenty-four chapters, while she had plans for twenty. She sent the twelve finished chapters off to Washington Street for reaction and in the meantime kept on writing. She also, while working on the book, had managed to write three short stories for other publishers. Frank Leslie was pestering her for stories also, but he would have to wait.

When word came back from Thomas Niles, it was unsettling. The manuscript was not what he had imagined; in fact, he found it dull. But, he admitted, he was a bachelor and didn't know girls well either. He had taken the liberty of passing Miss Alcott's manuscript on to his young niece for her reaction.

Louisa kept on writing. The story had taken her over. Beth's scarlet fever, the anxious days by her bedside, and John and Anna's love story went in, all against the back-

LOUISA MAY ALCOTT AT HER DESK IN ORCHARD HOUSE BEDROOM

ground of the Civil War. The tragicomic events of Louisa's own life became Jo's—the *Olive Branch* being renamed, wickedly, the *Spread Eagle,* and Louisa getting some of her own back against all the commonplace editors who had scorned her. Her own first story, "The Rival Painters," became Jo's first, and many of the plays the March girls performed had been written and performed by Louisa.

By July 15, all 402 pages were finished and Louisa was exhausted. May was busy working on illustrations. Her head aching constantly, Louisa bundled the balance of the manuscript off to Mr Niles and turned her attention to Abba, who was very feeble. She herself was close to physical breakdown.

Meanwhile, Thomas Niles had received the verdict from his niece and her friends. They loved the story, and please could they have more of it as soon as possible? Miss Alcott was invited to Washington Street to discuss contract terms. Thomas Niles, slender and scholarly and kindly eyed, explained that there was no way of knowing how well the book would do. It was, after all, something quite new. But it obviously had market appeal, and Miss Alcott had a following as the author of *Hospital Sketches* and the editor of *Merry's Museum*.

On behalf of Roberts Brothers, Niles had been authorized to offer Miss Alcott a choice of two contracts. She could have an advance of $300 against a royalty of 6.66 percent of the retail price of each copy sold. Or Roberts Brothers was prepared to buy the book outright, for the sum of $1,000, in which case she would be giving up all copyright claims and royalties. There was no guarantee that the book would even earn back a $300 advance. Mr. Niles then did a remarkable thing. Speaking as a friend, and going against his employer's own interests, he recommended that Louisa keep the copyright for herself.

There was still the question of a name for the book and for a second book to follow. Between them Louisa and Thomas Niles agreed on the title of Book I.

It would be called, they decided, *Little Women*.

EIGHTEEN

"The Miss Alcott"

LOUISA ENDED BOOK I of *Little Women* with Mr. March's first appearance, returning from the war, and Meg's engagement to John Brooke. "So . . . the curtain falls upon Meg, Jo, Beth, and Amy," she wrote in closing. "Whether it ever rises again, depends upon the reception given to the first act of the domestic drama called *Little Women*."

That was only half true. A month earlier she and Mr. Niles were already planning the sequel, which she suggested be called " 'Young Women,' or something of that sort."

To Louisa and her feminist friends, "little women" was an honorable phrase. It meant that the March sisters, in spite of their ages, were young *adults,* not little girls or even "young ladies." They had gone through great difficulties, just as the Alcott sisters had, and had grown in wisdom and compassion, responsibility and self-discipline.

Louisa didn't start on the sequel right away. She was still exhausted from writing Book I so quickly, and once it was finished she was caught up in household demands. Abba was "growing feeble," and Louisa was very worried about her. At the end of August the galley proofs of *Little Women* arrived.

"It reads better than I expected," Louisa admitted in her journal. Now she had the job of checking the proofs all through carefully for errors, corrections, and editorial changes she might not approve. Her old admirer and fellow actor George Bartlett, son of Concord's doctor, turned up at Orchard House, eager to be of service. Louisa squelched his romantic attempts. She had, she claimed, made up her mind to be an old maid. But she let him help with the proofreading.

In September 1868, Bronson's *Tablets* finally appeared in print, nineteen years after the summer of near madness in which it had been written. Now Bronson was a placid sixty-eight, and it was Louisa who went into a whirlwind to write books. Even though Roberts Brothers was really only publishing *Tablets* in order to keep Louisa as a Roberts author, it had done well by Bronson. The little book had a dignified brown cloth cover and gilt-edged pages. "Very simple outside, wise and beautiful within," Louisa recorded, adding a hope that it would bring her father profit and praise after his long wait.

Little Women made its debut at the end of September, its cover elegant with gilt lettering inside a gilt oval. Mr. Niles predicted it would have a great run. The book was out in time for Abba's sixty-eighth birthday, which the Alcotts celebrated in the old grand style. After breakfast Bronson escorted Abba to the big red chair in the study, where gifts were piled on the table. Her grandsons led the way with a flourish of trumpets, and Anna, Louisa, and May paraded at the rear. Abba was happy, but Louisa knew that for her mother the long decline had begun.

The reviews of *Little Women* began coming in, and they were good. Even more satisfying to Louisa was the praise of people she respected, like Thomas Higginson (the colonel of the first black regiment in the Union army) and his wife. By the end of October, Louisa knew that *Little Women* was a success. The first edition of two thousand copies was already sold out, another edition was underway, and a London publisher was rushing a British edition into print in time for Christmas. Could Miss Alcott write Book 2 by the first of the year, so it could be published in the spring? Miss Alcott would certainly try.

If she were going to do it, Louisa knew, she needed peace and quiet. Fortunately the Pratts had just moved into their new house in Malden, outside of Boston, and Abba and Bronson could board with them for the winter. Louisa took a room on Brookline Street, Boston, and began writing.

Her aim was to write a chapter a day and have the manuscript finished by the beginning of December. Success and fan mail, she found, were very inspirational. She looked into her memory and found the story easy to plan. It would begin with Meg's wedding, which would be Anna's wedding. May's artistic efforts, such as the pokerwork she had done on the Orchard House breadboard, and her own first experiences churning out potboilers, would provide funny scenes. The good and the bad of her trip to Europe as a companion could be transferred to Amy. The serious part of the story would come from the lessons in compromise, in reconciling dreams and practicality without sacrificing integrity, that she and her sisters had had to learn. But the tragic heart of it all would be Elizabeth's death. It was all in the journals and the letters Louisa had written home when she was away.

On one thing she was adamant from the first. "I *won't* marry Jo to Laurie to please any one," she wrote firmly in her journal on the same day she began writing the first chapter. Instead she created a man after her own heart. Professor Fritz Bhaer was German (Louisa loved German literature, and she admired Germany for standing by the Union during the Civil War). He had ideals but was not an idealist; he was a teacher and an intellectual but was not lost in the world of the mind. He had all of Bronson Alcott's good qualities, but also many that Bronson lacked—physical and emotional strength, sensitivity, compassion, a sense of responsibility toward those depending on him, a willingness to work at any honorable labor. Above all, he was a man who would respect Jo March as an equal partner.

On Sunday, November 1, Louisa plunged into her vortex. On the sixteenth she came up for air, having written "like a steam engine," and treated herself to lunch with three author friends. She also visited the Radical Club, to hear a speech on women's suffrage, and the New England Woman's Club. The next day she wrote the chapter in which Beth tells Jo she knows that she is dying. Louisa was deep in her vortex, skipping sleep and food, interrupting her writing only for a daily walk in Boston's cold autumn air.

Her birthday came. She spent it alone, lost in her writing. No presents came, except a copy of Bronson's *Tablets*. "I never seem to have many presents, as some do, though I give a good many," she noted wistfully, adding that it was probably for the best. The festive celebrations of her childhood were very far away.

December came with the book still unfinished. Louisa had to interrupt her writing to go back to Concord and close up Orchard House. Bronson was leaving on the eleventh on a winter-long lecture tour, and Abba was moving in with the

Pratts. "A cold, hard, dirty time; but was so glad to be off out of C. that I worked like a beaver, and turned the key on Apple Slump with joy," she commented.

She took May back with her to Boston. Dr. Dio Lewis, the gymnast who had had all Concord twisting itself into contortions some summers before, had taken a townhouse at 17 Beacon Street and turned it into a temperance (no alcohol served) hotel called the Bellevue. It was very elegant, with an elevator, a restaurant offering such delicacies as lobster salad and sherbet, an intercom system, and much marble. One of its special features was the bedrooms furnished like sitting rooms, with the beds converting into sofas by day, so that lady guests could entertain visitors respectably in their own private "parlors."

Louisa preferred quiet corners, but she knew how May hungered for style and glamour. They moved into a skyparlor at the Bellevue, where they enjoyed such modern conveniences as a gale that nearly blew the roof off and steam pipes that exploded. It was not what Louisa needed after a summer and autumn of hard work and with a manuscript yet to complete.

On New Year's Day Louisa sent *Little Women,* Book 2, off to Thomas Niles. Book 1 was doing very well, and she had received $300 in royalties on Christmas Day. She had totaled her earnings for 1868 and found they had come to more than $1,300. Publishers were begging her for her work, as editor, novelist, or writer of whatever she wished.

But she had paid a hard price for the success. The headaches, wracking cough, and weariness had set in again. They had plagued her off and on ever since those last terrible, cold months at Fruitlands, and had grown in force in the sick dampness of the Union Hotel Hospital. Now there was no more coldness, no more financial worries, but the cough and the pains were there like ghosts at a celebration feast. They were making her afraid, because they interfered with her ability to write. She wondered if she would be able to keep on editing *Merry's Museum,* or to start the next book that Roberts Brothers already wanted.

In January, to Louisa's relief, she and May moved to the quiet of a boardinghouse at 53 Chauncy Street. Between books, and struggling with headaches, she was still hard at work. There were business letters to write; she was learning to be a stern negotiator and stand up for her rights. She was able to write with satisfaction to Sam May that she had paid off all her father's debts and had even been able to send Cousin Samuel Sewall some money to invest for her. She was getting on well for a "shiftless Alcott," she told her uncle. Abba was happy at Anna's, Bronson was enjoying his lecture tour and *Tablets,* May was teaching art, and could Sam please send some more anecdotes or incidents out of May family memory? Louisa was under constant pressure for articles and stories, and she loved to draw on the Mays' long history in Boston.

In March Bronson and Abba returned to Concord. So did Louisa, leaving May in Boston for another two months. Louisa was still ill, her health so broken by now that her family was growing panic stricken. In June, Bronson wrote to a friend that Louisa's cough and bronchial troubles had persisted for six months, damaging both her temper and her ability to work.

Louisa was frightened. She knew she did her most successful work while "in a vortex," but she also knew her body would no longer take the punishment of fourteen-hour workdays and inability to sleep. To write "in a whirlwind" as Louisa did was exhausting—physically, emotionally, and mentally. Louisa had nightmares often, and relived the horrors of the hospital. She had suffered delirium for months in the aftermath of her war experience, and she remembered Bronson's two descents into insanity when driven by his overactive brain. Now she found herself scared to start a new book for fear of the vortex and the sickness that would follow.

Concord in blossoming spring should have been a restful change, but it was not. Louisa discovered to her chagrin that she was now "*the* Miss Alcott" who had written *Little Women* and was a "sight" on fans' "literary pilgrimages." Escaping autograph hounds had been easier in a Boston boardinghouse than it was on the Lexington Road. Reporters were haunting the woods around Orchard House. Louisa relieved her mind by writing a very funny letter, about Concord as a literary mecca, to the Springfield *Republican,* and signing it "Tribulation Periwinkle." She took to hiding out, as Nathaniel Hawthorne had done.

Merry's Museum needed a serial from Miss Alcott, and Thomas Niles was waiting for another book. Louisa went into the vortex again to write *An Old-Fashioned Girl.* This time she was, quite frankly, writing in a crusade for modern women and against the foolishness she saw young girls still being subjected to in the name of catching husbands and being in fashion. She turned the format of *Little Women* inside out. Instead of lonely, rich, orphaned Laurie being "adopted" by the poor but loving family circle of the Marches, *An Old-Fashioned Girl* was about life among the Boston bluebloods—and the new rich—as seen by an "old-fashioned country girl," Polly Milton (her last name borrowed from the author of *Paradise Lost*).

Polly, like Louisa, came from a poor but loving family with a wise, practical mother and a preacher father. Polly, too, loved the culture and excitement of the big city but was troubled by the shallowness, snobbishness, and false values she saw there. Like Louisa in her early Boston days as a "poor relation," she saw the condescension beneath the kindness and hated being patronized. Like Louisa, she longed for a real silk dress.

Abba appeared again in *An Old-Fashioned Girl*, not as the mother, but as a wise grandmother beside the fire, remembering the fun of her own schooldays, the life on Temple Place, and Great-Aunt Hancock, who had been kissed on the cheek by Lafayette. Polly Milton was neither Louisa May Alcott nor Jo March but a mixture of all the Alcott sisters. Like Elizabeth, she loved her music. Like Anna, she was gentle until pushed into stubbornness. Like May, she loved beautiful things and pretty clothes. Like Louisa, she believed in well-rounded, independent women who could look after themselves and those they loved. By now hoops were "out" and bustles were "in"; so were frizzed hair, bronze boots, and a lot of fads Louisa could take great delight in poking fun at. The serial concluded with Polly packing her trunk to go back to the country parsonage, with all characters having become wiser through her visit.

In July *An Old-Fashioned Girl* began serialization in *Merry's Museum* and Louisa escaped to Rivière du Loup, a small island in the St. Lawrence River outside Quebec, with cousins, and in August to Mount Desert, Maine, with May. All that autumn, the reviews and the sales of *Little Women*, Books 1 and 2, rolled in. So did fan letters, from boys and girls, men and women, distinguished persons. Meg, Jo, Beth, and Amy were being laughed and cried over even in college dormitories and faculty rooms.

In October, Louisa and May returned to Boston, to 43 Pinckney Street. In silk gowns trimmed with lace or tulle ruching, Louisa attended Sunday evening receptions, took tea at the New England Woman's Club with fellow members who included Julia Ward Howe, author of the "Battle Hymn of the Republic." Bronson, on his lecture tour, found himself billed as the "father of Miss L. M. Alcott" or the "Father of the Little Women."

The invitations and the money came rolling in. The only shadow was once again of sickness. That autumn Louisa's bronchial condition and cough were so severe that she was ordered to undergo the daily ordeal of having her "windpipe burnt with a caustic." For months she was forbidden to speak, and couldn't have anyhow.

Louisa's rheumatism was also raging in hand and foot. With her left arm in a sling and her leg propped up, taking potions to help her sleep, Louisa went back into the vortex to write the second half of *An Old-Fashioned Girl* so that Roberts Brothers would have a book-length manuscript to publish in the spring. This time, tongue in cheek, she pushed the story six years into the future, taking for granted that fads and fashions would be even more ridiculous by then. Polly was back in Boston, earning her living as a music teacher just as May was earning hers by teaching art. Circumstances had changed. Polly was no longer the guest of a society family but on her own, and the Shaw family was no longer rich. Quiet, long-suffering Mr. Shaw had been forced into an honorable bankruptcy, just as Grandfather May had been, because of the dishonesty of a friend whose debts he had guaranteed.

Now Louisa could write things she would have had difficulty getting published if she had not been "*the* Miss Alcott." She spoke bluntly about the scandal of girls being "sold" into loveless marriages for the sake of money, and of the plight of young girls alone in the city with no way to earn a living. Of the shame of a society that did not look after the neediest in its midst. All the things she had learned about from Abba's social work and at feminist meetings she brought out in *An Old-Fashioned Girl* and the books that followed.

Louisa also championed other controversial causes in *An Old-Fashioned Girl*: women's right to vote; their right to busy, independent, respected lives, married or unmarried; new kinds of families. Polly Milton was part of a sisterhood of gifted young women who used their talents to help others and support themselves.

Christmas Day brought a welcome shock—a royalty check for $2,500 for sales of *Little Women*. Louisa had become a wealthy woman. Bronson's debts were paid off, the Alcott Sinking Fund showed a healthy balance, and she had every prospect of continuing to earn good money so long as her health held out. The family was safe at last. It was time to think of herself and to fulfill a dream.

Dr. Bartlett's daughter Alice, now a lively and cultured young woman of twenty-four, was about to make a grand tour of Europe and wanted a traveling companion. Most particularly, she wanted *the* Miss Alcott. She invited May to come as her companion, on condition that Louisa would come also. Perhaps that provision persuaded Louisa to spend money on herself for a change.

Once again Louisa packed her trunk, but with a difference. This time she could have all the silk gowns she wished and travel where and how she wanted, secure in the knowledge that a welcome waited everywhere for the author of *Little Women*. On the first day of April, Louisa and May took the train for New York with John Pratt as their escort. A peddler boy on the train tried to sell Louisa a book to read.

"Bully book, ma'am! Sell a lot; better have it," he urged when Louisa said no.

The book was *An Old-Fashioned Girl,* just published, with an advance sale of 12,000 copies. John Pratt had the fun of telling the boy he was trying to sell the author her own book.

The next day, in a gale of wind, Louisa and May set sail with Alice Bartlett on the French steamer *Lafayette*.

All of Europe, it seemed, waited to welcome Louisa. For some time she had been in correspondence with European friends met on her earlier journey and with new friends made through *Little Women*. They spent several weeks in Brittany, with Louisa enjoying May's raptures. Everywhere, Louisa made notes and journal entries and wrote letters home, conscious she could use all these experiences in articles.

Their home base was a suite of rooms at Madame Coste's pension on the Place St. Louis in Dinon. A salon elegant with blue brocade; a bedroom for Alice; a larger one upstairs for May and Louisa, done in green French chintz! May sketched everything, and Louisa made notes of their fellow guests. Letters came from home, telling how well the new book was selling, how Miss Alcott's recent photograph (dignified in silk, suitable for autographing) was appearing everywhere.

Louisa's leg was still hurting, and she consulted a Dr. Kane, who had been an army surgeon in India. He was the first doctor to understand exactly what had happened to her in the Union Hotel Hospital, because he had suffered from the same thing. The calomel she had been given in large doses had contained mercury. "The bunches in my leg are owing to that, for the mercury lies around in a body and don't do much harm till a weak spot appears when it goes there and makes trouble," Louisa wrote home to Concord. She added that all she knew was that her leg was the curse of her life and that she thought Dr. Kane's prescription of iodine of potash would cure her condition, as it had his.

Dr. Kane was a rich, gray-haired bachelor, impressed with Louisa's military service, and Louisa was soon being teased about her new beau. The important thing was that by June she felt a lot better. She was sleeping, too, thanks to the sleeping draughts that had been prescribed back home and the pain pills Dr. Kane provided. Louisa was taking both morphine and opium, but she didn't know, as even the doctors didn't know, that both were addictive drugs. In 1870 both were regarded as miracle pain-relievers.

In midsummer the travelers moved on to Blois and from there to Geneva, Switzerland, and then to Vevey. The letters flew back and forth across the Atlantic. Louisa was not only writing to her family, she was settling business matters with publishers and explaining to editors that she was on vacation and could not keep obliging them with more stories. Actually, she was storing up material for later use, and she shortly ran into more excitement than she had bargained for.

Trouble between France and Germany had been building up for some time. On the nineteenth of July, war broke out. Refugees began streaming into Vevey. It was a terrible time for France. Paris was under siege, and even the zoo animals were being killed and eaten. On the second of September, the French emperor Napoleon III surrendered to Germany.

"[A]ll Europe seems to be going to destruction," Louisa wrote home to her anxious family eight days later. She, May, and Alice Bartlett meant to cross the Alps into Italy the following week, if war and the weather permitted. They planned to visit Milan and the Italian lake district, then settle down in Rome for the winter.

October in Italy was heavenly. By November they were in Rome, and May was in an artist's heaven. Louisa was feeling the cold and damp, for Rome was wet with steady rain. She also found the dirt and decay depressing. But their six-room apartment on the Piazza Barberini was warm, and they had hired a maid to cook and clean. Louisa's thirty-eighth birthday came and was celebrated in style. They were looking forward to a Roman Christmas.

On December 23, Louisa picked up an English-language newspaper and read that John Pratt was dead.

NINETEEN

"Hints of a Woman Early Old"

JOHN BRIDGE PRATT, whom she had first resented and now loved as her brother, was gone.

"[F]ill my place a little till I come," Louisa begged Cousin Lizzie Wells, who had been one of the first to go to Anna. Louisa's heart was anxious about Abba as well as Anna, but winter, her own health, and other matters prevented her from going home at once. Over that sad Christmas Louisa grieved, then sat down to do the one thing she alone could do. She wrote a book for Anna and her boys, so they would have income in addition to the money that John had carefully put aside for them.

Rome was festive with holiday celebrations, then in an uproar as the Tiber overflowed its banks. The city's gas streetlights went out, thieves took advantage of the dark, and Louisa, May, and Alice armed themselves with a pistol, two daggers, and one umbrella. Victor Emmanuel, king of an only recently united Italy, came to view the damage. The pre-Lenten carnival began. In the apartment on the Piazza Barberini, Louisa picked up her pen, finding comfort in "writing and thinking of the little lads, to whom I must be a father now." She was writing not only for, but about, her "dear boys." Out of her memories of them and of John, her respect for Bronson's misunderstood educational ideas, and her own classroom experiences, she created a new kind of school, one that "Mrs. Jo" and Professor Bhaer would run at Plumfield, Aunt March's old home. She called the book *Little Men*.

While in Rome, Louisa sat for her portrait by the fashionable society painter George Healy. Healy's daughter was an author, and Louisa was generous with professional advice. In gratitude Healy gave her the portrait—the literary lion in lace-trimmed black silk, seated in a chair of red brocade.

Moods, Louisa's first "real" novel, suddenly began selling again on the strength of *the* Miss Alcott's new popularity. Seven hundred dollars in royalties from it came in, and Louisa decided to use the money to provide another year of European study for May. During the spring of 1871, Louisa, May, and Alice Bartlett traveled through Italy and then through the Alps to Germany, Belgium, and at last London. Louisa had promised her publishers to be available there when the British edition of *Little Men* was published on May 15. She booked passage on the *Malta,* sailing for the United States ten days later. It had been what she called a "very pleasant year in spite of constant pain," and a useful one for May. But now she was needed at home.

This time there was no John Pratt to meet her at the Boston pier, but Thomas Niles was there, and so was Bronson. It was publication day for the American edition of *Little*

Men. A huge red placard advertising the book adorned their carriage. Fifty thousand copies had been sold in advance.

At the Orchard House her family waited. Anna had a heartbreaking sweet calmness, and the boys had grown. Freddy was eight already, and Johnny would have his sixth birthday in three weeks. Abba, to Louisa's eyes, was much more feeble. Bronson's winter tour had been a success, and the Alcotts had refurnished and decorated Louisa's room out of his earnings.

In spite of the sadness over John's absence, June was a happy month. For the first time in two years, Louisa felt really well. She made the most of it, knowing it wouldn't last.

It didn't. From July through September 1871, there was too much to do and too many guests. Letters from publishers, fan mail, and the fans themselves kept arriving. Sam May, the last of Abba's brothers and sisters, died. All this, added to the heat and humidity of the Massachusetts summer, upset Louisa's nerves again, or so she thought. Actually the climate probably brought on her rheumatism, and the morphine she was taking again for pain caused the reaction the doctors labeled "nerves."

By October she had faced the fact that life in Concord was too hard for her. Louisa hired two women to do the housework, left plenty of money for household expenses, and fled to the ordered peace of a boardinghouse at 23 Beacon Street. There, at last, her bones ached less and she was able to give up the morphine. The celebrated Miss Alcott had returned to Boston, an elegant woman in black silk with a black velvet ribbon binding the thick braided chignon of graying chestnut hair. She had, like her mother, become graceful and stately in maturity, and her fine eyes had more of the Mays about them than ever.

Louisa was settling back into the pattern of life that worked well for her, in spite of her physical pain. Rest, lectures, concerts, galleries and museums . . . social events with interesting, cultured people . . . writing as much as she could without risk of "brain fever," and attending to business . . . and public service. Now that Louisa had so much money that she could take time from constant writing, and a name that commanded attention, she began speaking out often for the causes she believed in, especially the improvement of conditions for the freed slaves, and women's suffrage. And better ways of education. She had begun "preaching" about that in *Little Men,* and she did not mean to stop.

In November 1871, Louisa sent for May. May's eyes were troubling her, and in Louisa's opinion a spell of being the Orchard House housekeeper would do May good and give her eyes a rest. May arrived, willingly, in time for Louisa's thirty-ninth birthday, Bronson's seventy-second. For the first time in years, it was celebrated "in the old way." The Alcotts and the Pratts ate Thanksgiving dinner together at Pickle Roost, feeling, in spite of everything, that they had much to be thankful for.

"A varied, but on the whole a good year, in spite of pain," Louisa summed up 1871 at its end. She was feeling better in body and mind. May was lifting spirits and running things in Concord, where Louisa had installed central heating to replace the old picturesque open fires. Louisa was being made much of in Boston, where she had gone to a ball for Grand Duke Alexis of Russia. Christmas at Orchard House was celebrated with a tree, a family dinner, and an evening frolic.

Her royalty payments in January 1872 came to more than four thousand dollars. Louisa invested three thousand and put the rest in the bank for family needs. She was rich and famous, and an unknown admirer was sending her huge bouquets daily. Harriet Beecher Stowe asked her to write something for the *Christian Union*, and Louisa provided "Shawl Straps," an account of her travels through France. She was trying to preserve her health by not working or playing too much.

"Much talk about religion," Louisa commented after attending lectures. "I'd like to see a little more really *lived*." She wrote another travel article, this time for the *Independent*, and the fee paid her winter's expenses. "All is fish that comes to the literary net," she noted. "Goethe puts his joys and sorrows into poems; I turn my adventures into bread and butter." She was gaining a reputation in the nonfiction field. It wasn't necessary to go into a vortex to write these pieces; all she had to do was edit and annotate her travel notes, journal entries, and letters home.

In 1852 she had resolved to make the family independent and free of financial worry. Now, twenty years later, she had done it. It had cost Louisa her health, but she had survived.

She went back to Concord for the summer and was again plagued by autograph seekers. "People *must* learn that authors have some rights; I can't entertain a dozen a day, and write the tales they demand also. . . . Reporters sit on the wall and take notes; artists sketch me as I pick pears in the garden; and strange women interview Johnny as he plays in the orchard. It looks like impertinent curiosity to me, but it is called 'fame,' and considered a blessing to be grateful for, I find. Let 'em try it!"

In September, Bronson took Louisa and Freddy to Spindle Hill to show them his boyhood home. It gave Louisa ideas for a boys' book she hoped one day to write about her father. In October she was back in Boston, this time at 7 Allston Street, expanding "Shawl Straps" to book length for Roberts

Brothers. A month later she was buying new clothes and a new trunk for Bronson and speeding him off for the West and another lecture tour.

The *Christian Union* asked again for a serial story, this time offering three thousand dollars. Louisa dug out her old manuscript of *Success,* now renamed *Work,* and plunged into her vortex, wondering if she would ever be able to get out again. Roberts Brothers and Low of London heard what Miss Alcott was doing and begged for the privilege of publishing *Work* in book form. Miss Alcott gave in and began writing the manuscript in triplicate, pressing down hard with her pen to make the carbon copies legible. She permanently destroyed the gripping power of her thumb in the process and had to teach herself to write without the use of her thumb or with her other hand.

Louisa's income for the year was over nine thousand dollars, and her public was clamoring for more to read. Now she had a new responsibility—not to her family, but to her readers, especially the young.

The writing went well, but Louisa was going at it slowly for fear of breakdown. Anna almost died of pneumonia in 1873, and Louisa nursed her. When *Work* was completed, Louisa sent May back to London and took her place in Concord. Anna was living with her in-laws at Pickle Roost. Abba was very ill with heart trouble and dropsy, and her brain was affected. After three weeks the "mental bewilderment" eased a little, but she would never be the same. In November, Louisa scooped up her mother, Anna, and the boys and took them all to Boston, to a boardinghouse at 26 East Brookline Street. It was a joy to drive Abba around her old city, but Boston was Louisa's city now, not Abba's.

The weight of family was heavy on Louisa's shoulders. Abba was very sick again in January 1874, and both mother and daughter knew it was the beginning of the end. Bronson was feeling blue, and left out of the limelight in philosophical circles. "A little more money, a pleasant house and time to attend to it, and I'd bring all the best people to see and entertain *him*," Louisa wrote with evident frustration. "When I had the youth I had no money; now I have the money I have no time; and when I get the time, if I ever do, I shall have no health to enjoy life. . . . [I]t's rather hard to love the things I do and see them go by because duty chains me to my galley." If she was giving in briefly to bitterness, she had earned the right.

May came home in early spring, happy with the praise her work had received in London's artistic circles. Louisa was able to return to Boston for the spring. Summer meant a return to Concord, and then to Conway, New Hampshire, with Anna and the boys. Louisa had been sick a good deal during the year, and the fresh air and fun at the Atherton farm did her good. "How I Went out to Service," Louisa's account of her Dedham experience, was finally published that June. The *Independent* paid her $200 for the privilege. During the summer, Louisa began writing the serial that Mary Mapes Dodge had been demanding for *St. Nicholas,* bearing in mind that Mrs. Dodge didn't want anything "preachy."

Louisa felt like preaching—about the reformation of the American educational system—but she could do it most effectively with humor. So she created a family compound nicknamed Aunt Hill, where a lot of aunts, uncles, and boy cousins lived in nearby homes. In their midst she set down a bachelor uncle and his orphaned niece and ward, whose name was Rose. As with *An Old-Fashioned Girl,* Louisa made her readers laugh with her at the ridiculous customs of fashionable society and see the wisdom of sensible food and lots of exercise. As with *Little Men,* she gloried in a world of boys. She called the new book *Eight Cousins.*

1875 was a very good year. Bronson was traveling through the West, "riding in Louisa's chariot, and adored as the grandfather of 'Little Women,' " as he wrote home proudly. Louisa was invited to be an honored guest at the tenth anniversary of Vassar College, a pioneering educational institution for women. She paid a visit to New York City, and went home to Concord for the grand celebrations of the hundredth anniversary of the "shot heard round the world." Mr. Emerson unveiled the bronze Minuteman statue by the sculptor Daniel Chester French. May Alcott had been one of his first teachers.

Summer came, with more lion hunters looking for Louisa. The Alcotts entertained ninety-two guests in a single month, and Louisa decided fame was the greatest mess she had ever gotten herself into.

In the autumn she packed her silk gowns and small fashionable bonnets, her manuscripts and pen, and moved to New York City. Dr. Eli Peck Miller, a colleague of Dr. Dio Lewis, had opened a spa hotel at 39 West 26th Street, similar to the Bellevue in Boston. Amid the brownstones of fashionable New York and the old brick Federal townhouses, the bustle of the splendid stores and the glittering drawing rooms, New York's literary establishment welcomed *the* Miss Alcott with open arms and a round of parties. Louisa thoroughly enjoyed the social whirl, but she spent Christmas Day helping a Quaker couple spread cheer at an orphans' home.

The best parts of 1875 for Louisa were her many visits to the theater, and the fact that she had hardly been sick at all.

In America's centennial year, 1876, Louisa went to the Centennial Ball at Boston's Music Hall. She skipped the exposition in Philadelphia, writing tartly that "America ought to pay her debts before she gives parties." For Louisa the year was one of dullness, not celebration. In February she went to the Bellevue and tried to write, but book ideas failed her. She went back to Orchard House to nurse Abba and stayed there for the summer, cleaning house with May while Anna and the boys visited at Pickle Roost.

Louisa was trying to "get up steam" for another serial for Mrs. Dodge; it would pay well, but she was out of inspiration. Roberts Brothers wanted a novel. Newspapers and magazines were demanding tales. "My brain is squeezed dry," Louisa confessed to her journal, "and I can only wait for help." By the end of summer she had her book idea, though she had to push it off until September, for she was getting May ready for another year abroad. On the ninth, May sailed on the *China*. On the twenty-sixth, Louisa sent the final chapters of the new manuscript to Mrs. Dodge. She had written a sequel to *Eight Cousins* in less than four weeks. *Rose in Bloom* continued the themes she had spoken out on in *Eight Cousins* and *An Old-Fashioned Girl*, and went even farther. Rose Campbell, the wealthy heiress, devoted herself to a career of philanthropy, to the dismay and amusement of her social set. She had to learn the difference between haphazard "do-gooding" and sensible social work, and between love built only on passion and love that also included common sense, companionship, and respect. *Rose in Bloom* came out in book form, in England and America, within two months of its writing.

Three times, in summing up the year in her journal, Louisa used the word *dull*.

The year 1877 promised better things. At Orchard House Anna was housekeeper, the boys were growing, Bronson was writing *Table-Talk*, and Abba was busy too with reading, sewing, writing letters, and reveling in her girls' success. Louisa could take off for the Bellevue with a light heart. She had an idea for a different sort of novel, definitely for adults. Roberts Brothers was publishing what was called its No Name Series. The books, by known authors, were all published anonymously, and readers had the fun of trying to guess the authors.

Louisa's plot was inspired by Goethe's dramatic poem about Dr. Faustus, who fell hopelessly in love with a pure and beautiful woman and sold his soul to the devil in order to win her. The ghost of "A. M. Barnard" was stirring in Louisa. She could write this allegory for adults in the lush language and imagery of thrillers, rather than in the simpler sentences and everyday language—even slang—she had pioneered in *Little Women*. But Louisa was now twenty years older than A. M. Barnard had been, and her writing had more depth and wisdom. She wrote about crime and punishment, and the struggle between good and evil for a human soul.

Louisa named her book *A Modern Mephistopheles*. No one but Abba and Anna knew about it. She had even had Anna and another woman copy the manuscript for her, so Thomas Niles would not recognize the handwriting.

A Modern Mephistopheles was published in April, to high praise. Spring lengthened into summer, and Bronson's *Table-Talk* came out in print. With the book finished, Louisa returned to considering her family's needs. Anna missed having a home of her own, and Orchard House was becoming too much of a responsibility for them all. The old Thoreau house on Main Street, in Concord, was on the market, and Louisa proposed adding $2,500 to the $2,000 Anna had available from John Pratt's savings. She had the money from her railroad investments, Louisa pointed out, and if Anna could look after Abba during the winters—in a home of her own—

things would go more smoothly, and Louisa would be free to write in Boston. Concord held nothing for Louisa anymore. Where she really wanted to go was back to Europe, but she didn't see how she could. Abba was failing again, in spite of looking forward to the new house, in spite of cheery letters of May's successes and pleasant drives with Louisa and Anna through the Concord woods.

Louisa herself was feeling well and beginning to hope she had conquered her illness. By late summer she had overworked herself again and was laid up for weeks, resting quietly. *Under the Lilacs,* a serial she had "owed" Mrs. Dodge for a long time, was beginning to jell in her brain. She began writing it, a little at a time.

The pleasant times ended with a lurch on the seventh of September. Abba had a bad turn, so bad that Bronson, who was at Spindle Hill, had to be summoned home. The doctor told Louisa that the end was coming, and Abba herself longed for her suffering to be over. Again, Louisa threw herself into nursing, writing stories while she watched at her mother's side and, somehow, finishing *Under the Lilacs.* She could see a bad winter coming.

In October, Louisa's own health was breaking down. She brought a nurse in to care for Abba, so that she herself would be well enough to stand by Abba when her last hours came. "Stand by and help me if I suffer too much," Abba begged. Louisa promised, but there was little she could do except watch her mother struggle for breath day after day. Abba's seventy-seventh birthday came. They had a sad celebration. Then, as always when Louisa neglected her own health, she herself fell terribly ill. For a week she lay near death and "feared to go before Marmee. But pulled through, and got up slowly to help her die. A strange month," she wrote in her journal after it was over.

Abba's illness, and Louisa's, had put off the move to the Thoreau house, Anna's house now. But Abba insisted the move take place, just as she insisted that May not be called home. On the fourteenth of November, they walked out of Orchard House for the last time. Abba was carried upstairs to her new bedroom in her armchair, murmuring with a smile, "This is the beginning of my ascension."

For weeks now Abba had spent day and night in her chair, unable to struggle for breath when lying down. After a week in the new home Abba took to her bed. For three days she lay there, surrounded by flowers and sunshine and the family that she loved, slipping in and out of consciousness. At one point on Saturday she looked at a picture on the wall, recognized it, and waved. "Goodbye, little May, goodbye!"

On Sunday, November 25, the winter rain fell, and Abba's mind wandered back to the happy days at Temple Court. She was a young girl again, calling Louisa "Mother." "A smile is as good as a prayer," she murmured. At dusk Abba May Alcott drew her last tired breath in her daughter Louisa's arms.

ABIGAIL MAY ALCOTT IN STUDY OF ORCHARD HOUSE

TWENTY

" A Woman in a Lonely Home "

THAT SAME DAY, Louisa sat down to write to May the account of Abba's last hours. On Tuesday they laid Abba away beside Elizabeth in the winter sunset. On Wednesday a small service was held at Anna's home. For Louisa there was a great emptiness, and a great loss of warmth. "Help me," Abba had murmured. And Louisa had. In the thirty-four years since Fruitlands, Louisa had devoted her life to her family. Now she was more free, but the freedom brought no joy into her grief and physical pain.

"[T]here is no motive to go on now," Louisa wrote bleakly. "I think I shall soon follow her."

The year ended, and 1878 began. Bronson wandered around Concord like a lost soul. Louisa tried to write about her mother's life, but could not. ("[N]o one understood all she had to bear but we, her children," she told her journal.)

Instead she wrote a poem called "Transfiguration," which was published later in the year.

Far away in London, May was grieving. As Amy, far off in Switzerland when Beth died, had been comforted by Laurie, so May was comforted by a new friend, and sorrow drew them into love. His name was Ernest Nieriker, and he was a Swiss banker. He was also only twenty-two to May's thirty-seven, but that bothered neither of them. He was mature and tender, and in adulthood May still retained the gracefulness and charm of her girlhood. In February 1878 they became engaged, to the happiness and good wishes of both families.

On March 22, May Alcott of Concord, Massachusetts, became Madame Nieriker of London, Paris, and Baden, Switzerland. The marriage took place in a London registry office, and May wore a brown silk gown and a hat with plumes.

Letters full of happiness flew across the Atlantic. The newlyweds honeymooned in France, where Ernest had business to attend to. He wrote respectfully to his new father-in-law. May begged Louisa to come visit. She and Ernest had taken a house in Meudon, France, with a balcony and garden. She was busy with her art, and she and her husband spent the evenings reveling in music.

Back in Concord, Anna cleared out the remaining furnishings in Orchard House, and she and Louisa began seeking a tenant for it. For a while Louisa drifted, sick in heart and body. Slowly, she began to come back to life. She and Bronson began going through the papers and journals Abba had left behind. Abba had left her journals to Louisa, wanting them destroyed but trusting her daughter's judgment. She had signed the letter of instructions "Marmee." Thomas Niles had promised to publish any memoir Louisa should write, but she couldn't do it.

By July Louisa knew she was improving fast. She planned

to sail to Europe in September but at the last minute became afraid the trip would be too much for her. That was a good thing; Anna broke her leg and needed Louisa's care.

It had been a strange year. By its end Louisa could write that things were looking up and all was well. A new project, spurred on by Louisa, was in the thinking stage—a School of Philosophy, at which Bronson could teach the fruits of his wisdom to adult disciples. Boston might not find him worth listening to, but the young and old he had met on his western travels did.

January of 1879 found Louisa back at the Bellevue writing. She started two books, but kept putting off plunging into a vortex. Instead she went about visiting, to meetings and concerts and charity events. One of these was a Carnival of Authors at the Music Hall. Miss Alcott presented *Mrs. Jarley's Waxworks*, wearing a short green gown, pink stockings, a red shawl, a cape-sized collar, and a bonnet that, according to one newspaper report, was "enough to throw a modern milliner into convulsions." Not for nothing had Louisa been the family milliner. Her triumph on this occasion was of green silk lined with pink, with a rampant feather, and she wore it perched on hair rolled in puffs on either side of wire-rimmed spectacles.

In spite of all this gaiety, Louisa was tired. She went back to Anna's in February, feeling used up. She had invested $1,000 for each of her nephews' education. Now she wanted to build up her health and rest in hope of sailing for Paris in the spring. The Nierikers were still in a honeymoon haze, to the wonder of European neighbors who gossiped over their differences of age and background. May wanted to share her happiness with her famous sister.

Back and forth the letters went. Louisa had much to tell her sister. *The* Miss Alcott was still being lionized in Boston.

She and author Frances Hodgson Burnett were guests of honor at a Papyrus Club dinner meeting at the Revere House. Oliver Wendell Holmes himself took Louisa in to dinner, and toasts were drunk to *Little Women*. Louisa entertained Mrs. Burnett, her son (who had been the model for *Little Lord Fauntleroy*), and Mary Mapes Dodge for lunch in Concord.

Anna celebrated her forty-eighth birthday in March. "The best woman I know," Louisa called her, "always reasonable, just, kind, & forgiving. . . . A good sister to me all these years in spite of the utter unlikeness of our tastes, temperaments & lives. If we did not love one another so well we never could get on at all. As it is I am a trial to her & she to me sometimes, our views are so different." That was one of the greatest things Louisa had learned from her family; perhaps the greatest thing she was able to pass on to young readers through her books. *Family* didn't mean liking, or loving, one another all the time. *Family* was a bond that went far deeper. And, as she demonstrated constantly in *Little Men, An Old-Fashioned Girl,* and other pieces, being family didn't have to depend on blood ties either.

To Louisa's dismay, the aches of rheumatism, and the aches caused by the mercury left in her body from the calomel, returned. "Very poorly and cross. So tired of being a prisoner to pain," Louisa wrote bluntly in April. Even then her sense of humor surfaced. "Having overworked the wonderful machine I must pay for it, & should not growl I suppose as it is just."

She visited her friend Dr. Rhoda Lawrence, who not long before had graduated from the Boston University School of Medicine. Dr. Lawrence told Louisa frankly that she was much better than could have been expected, and she need not worry. Louisa's legs were so bad she couldn't walk much, but she bought a phaeton so that she and Bronson could go for carriage rides around Concord. Bronson enjoyed that, and he loved taking his many guests about. In his old age he was becoming as much a "sight" to out-of-town visitors as his daughter was.

Louisa's trip to France was postponed, not only because of her health but for a happier reason. May was expecting a baby in the autumn, and Louisa wanted to be there when the child was born.

Louisa had too much May stubbornness to give in to sickness except when absolutely necessary. She might weep or rage to her journal, but what the world saw was a famous author devoting herself more and more to good causes and social welfare crusades. One Sunday she went with Bronson to visit the new state prison in West Concord. Four hundred male faces stared back at her after Bronson's sermon. The least she could do was amuse them, so she told a lively story of her hospital days.

Another cherished dream came true that summer. Bronson's School of Philosophy opened in the study of Orchard House, which was lent back to him by the summer tenants. It began with thirty pupils. Concord had found it all a great joke, but Westerners came hundreds of miles to hear Bronson Alcott—and soon the town swarmed with eager philosophers. Eventually a separate building had to be put up to house the growing school.

In 1879, for the first time, women in Concord were allowed to register to vote. Louisa was the first to register her name. Between the School of Philosophy and other visitors Louisa was swamped all summer, but she did manage to write some and to get away to the shore for a week with her friend Laura Hosmer. In September she started a new serial for Mrs. Dodge. She had no real plans for it, except that it would be about the boys and girls of Concord. It was two years since she had written a full-length book, and she meant to take more time than usual. To Louisa that meant writing only one chapter a day.

By the end of October she had finished eight chapters. She was back to her favorite storyline from *Little Women*—friendship between boy and girl, rich and poor. Jill was much like Jo in many ways, but she had no sisters and no father. Jack had a studious brother and a wise and wealthy mother. Both were part of a large, lively crowd of schoolmates. Louisa started the story off with a bang—literally, for the sled carrying Jack and Jill down a steep coasting hill crashed into a tree. Jack's leg was broken (Louisa had Anna's experience to draw on there) and Jill's back was so hurt that she had to lie in a bed of pain for months, learning patience all the while. Louisa had her own experiences to draw on for that. She was not able to go to France after all, for her ailments were so bad again that she was told it was not safe for her to travel. She herself realized it would not be fair to inflict an invalid on her sister during her last months of pregnancy, no matter how much May begged her to come.

In November Louisa went back to the Bellevue, where she could finish *Jack and Jill* in peace and quiet. The story would be serialized in *St. Nicholas* between December 1879 and October 1880 and then be published in book form by Roberts Brothers. She was anxious about May, for thirty-eight was then considered old for bearing a first baby. But soon Louisa was able to record with relief that her namesake, Louisa May Nieriker, had been born in Paris at 9:00 A.M. on November 8, and all were doing well.

The happy news brightened the dark November days, for Louisa herself was not doing well at all. Since she couldn't write, she gave up her room at the Bellevue and went home

Nancy Hill-Joroff

FREDERICK ALCOTT PRATT AND JOHN SEWALL PRATT, C. 1870

Nancy Hill-Joroff

LOUISA MAY NIERIKER ("LULU"), C. 1883

in time for her birthday. If she were going to lie around, she decided, she could do it more cheaply in Concord than in Boston!

Louisa had a peculiar feeling that something was wrong, and very soon the mail from Paris confirmed her suspicions. Lulu, as the Nierikers called the baby in the French fashion, was doing fine, but May was not. Louisa's heart ached, but there was nothing she could do but hope and wait.

On the last day of the year, while Anna was off in Boston and Bronson had gone to the post office in hope of mail, Emerson arrived at Anna's house. Louisa found him standing before May's portrait, his face marked with tears.

May was dead, of meningitis. Even in his grief, Ernest Nieriker had thought to cable not the Alcotts but Emerson, so an old friend could break the news to the father and sisters May had left behind.

Louisa had the hard task of breaking the news, in turn, to Bronson and to Anna. She herself was overcome with grief. She had had premonitions, and she should have listened to them. She should have gone to May, however great the cost to her own health. She could not forgive herself that May had died with none of her blood kin near.

" 'Two years of perfect happiness' May called those married years, & said, 'If I die when baby comes dont mourn for I have had as much happiness in this short time as many in twenty years.' " But Louisa did mourn. The grieving widower had his new daughter to comfort him. But what comfort, Louisa wondered, was there for the Alcotts?

She was soon to learn. Letters came, telling that May had left her pictures and her baby daughter to Louisa.

On September 19, 1880, Louisa stood on the Boston wharf where she had seen May off to London three years earlier. The last sight Louisa had ever had of May was her standing alone on deck, her blue cloak blowing as she waved goodbye, her eyes wet although she smiled. Now Louisa waited not for May, but for her ten-month-old child.

At last the captain came ashore, followed by the woman Louisa had sent to fetch the baby, and Ernest Nieriker's teenage sister Sophie. In the captain's arms was "a little yellow haired thing in white, with its hat off as it looked about with lively blue eyes."

Louisa held out her arms.

TWENTY-ONE

"Brave Music"

TEN YEARS EARLIER, when John Pratt died, Louisa had vowed to be a "father" to his boys. She liked boys, she understood them and they all adored her. Johnny and Freddy were strapping teenagers now, a credit to their mother and their "Aunt Weedy." Actually, Louisa had been the unacknowledged head of the Alcott family for many years. Now, at nearly forty-eight, she was suddenly a mother. And to a girl, at that! But Lulu Nieriker was a girl after Louisa's own heart. She had May's charm and golden hair, and all Louisa's own stubbornness and independence. Louisa fell head over heels in love with her.

All of Concord was eager to see "Miss Alcott's baby." But Louisa had had enough of small-town living. She rented Cousin Lizzie Wells's house at 81 Pinckney Street and moved to town for the winter, taking the Pratt boys and Sophie

Nieriker with her, as well as Lulu and her nurse, Mrs. Giles. By November 10 Louisa was writing an account of Lulu's first birthday celebration to Bronson, who was on the lecture road again. "The little queen in her high chair sat & looked with delight at the tiny cake with *one* candle burning in it, picture books, flowers, a doll, silver mug, rattle with bells, & some gay cards. . . . She seemed quite over powered by her feelings & sung, laughed, called 'Up! Bow wow, Mama Da,' & all her little words, in great glee. Then she chose the picture book & was absorbed by it like a true artist's baby." Lulu even wore a "green crown" on her birthday, in the old Alcott tradition.

Louisa's life was taken up with her new daughter. "Too busy to keep much of a journal," she wrote in December, then added two sentences later, "On the 23rd she got up & walked alone. Had never crept at all, but when ready ran across the room & plumped down, laughing triumphantly at her feat." Lulu brought new life to all the Alcotts, who were still grieving for May.

The only thing that competed with Lulu for Louisa's attention was her reform work. "Yours for reform," she signed letters frequently throughout the 1880s. Louisa had been raised, as her mother had before her, to believe in private charity and helping the less fortunate. Like Abba, she had come to see there were limits to what individual people and individual pocketbooks could do. Now she could use her publicity value to try to raise other people's consciousness.

Louisa voted in the Concord school committee election of 1881 and tried to interest the Concord ladies in forming a suffrage club. During the summer she took Lulu and the boys to Nonquitt, Massachusetts. Lulu's fat little legs tramped around the broad porches of the hotel as she beamed at all the gentlemen. John and Fred dazzled the young ladies while boating or dancing. The "first old lady of Concord," as Louisa called herself, sat under her red parasol in her black silk dress and listened to the Marion Brass Band, or enjoyed theatricals or games of charades. As Boston had become Louisa's winter home, Nonquitt became the summer one for herself and her young people. She was too busy with Lulu to write books, but she did write short stories, and prefaces to a book of prayers by Theodore Parker and a new edition of *Moods*.

In April of 1882, Louisa tackled a sad responsibility. She reread Abba's diaries and destroyed most of them, sure she would never want strangers reading her own journals either.

Someday, Louisa promised herself, she would write a story or memoir about her mother's life. But for now there was Lulu, who was teething and wanted the comfort of Aunt Wee's arms, and there were the aches and pains that were making themselves known again in Louisa's weary body. Taking care of a toddler, even with a nurse to help, was exhausting for the woman whose health had been destroyed by the war and who was already of grandmother age.

The shadow of sadness was again spreading over the Alcotts. Emerson, who had been failing in health and mind, died on April 27. "The nearest & dearest friend father has ever had, & the man who has helped me most by his life, his books, his society. I can never tell all he has been to me. . . . Illustrious & beloved friend, goodbye!" Louisa wrote.

Summer brought better times. In July the School of Philosophy opened again, with glittering success. Anna's house was deluged with visitors wanting to pay respects to Bronson Alcott. "Several hundred a month is rather wearing," Louisa wrote in her journal. "Father asked why we never went" to the school sessions, and "Annie showed him a long list of 400 names of callers, & he said no more."

By autumn Louisa was back at the Bellevue, which had been converted into an apartment hotel. The boys went with her, for John was attending Chauncy Hall school and Fred was studying at the Conservatory of Music, majoring in piano and flute. Lulu was left in Concord with Anna. "Missed my dear baby, but need quiet," Louisa wrote. She was starting a new serial for Mrs. Dodge. It was to wrap up the saga of the March family and would be named *Jo's Boys*. Autumn promised well. Louisa even bought herself a new wardrobe, which she pronounced "very snappy."

On October 24 Bronson was struck with a paralytic stroke that affected both his body and his mind.

Louisa rushed to Concord to be with him and found him in very bad shape. In November she gave up her apartment at the Bellevue and moved home again to once more do her duty. It seemed unlikely Bronson would live long.

"Poor father, dumb & helpless! feeble mind slowly coming back. He knows us, but lies asleep most of the time. Get a nurse & wait to see if he will rally." Bronson had given fifty lectures at the School of Philosophy during the summer and the previous winter had written forty *Sonnets and Canzonets*, many of them love poems to his dead wife. Now he was, in Louisa's words, a "pathetic wreck."

Louisa was fifty that autumn, and Lulu a happy three. Bronson was eighty-three. "[P]oor father pays the penalty of breaking the laws of health," Louisa wrote. "I have done the same, may I be spared this end!"

Bronson came back from the land of the unconscious, but he would never again be as he had been. He had all the side effects of stroke—bouts of emotion, an inability to speak clearly—combined with his own temperament and old age. Louisa hired nurses, found them incompetent, and ended up doing much of the work herself.

When she could, she escaped to Boston or to Nonquitt, but she could never stay long. She and Anna shared the household responsibilities and took turns on duty. *Jo's Boys* was not progressing. Louisa started a novel called *Genius*. "Shall never finish it I dare say, but must keep a vent for my fancies to escape at. This double life is trying & my head will work as well as my hands."

Bronson was "hard to take care of being unreasonable, fretful & weak," she wrote. Lulu was four, and becoming a handful. "Love & patience are needed with a child like L. Force & indifference make her naughty. I can always manage her." Louisa could handle Lulu because Lulu was Louisa all over again.

"New Year's day is made memorable by my solemnly *spanking* my child. . . . She proudly says, 'Do it, do it!' & when it is done is heart broken at the idea . . . the effect, as I expected, a failure. Love is better, but also endless patience," Louisa wrote at the beginning of 1884. Soon Lulu began attending kindergarten for two hours a day. Fred's twenty-first birthday came. Louisa put $1,000 in the bank for him and bought him a dress suit.

She was trying to write, and turning out some stories, but her arm was lame. She tried electric-shock therapy, one of the latest medical treatments. In June another link with the past dissolved when Orchard House was sold. Louisa was not sorry to see it go; for her it had never been home. She bought herself a house at Nonquitt, where all was cool and quiet. Louisa spent June and July there with Lulu, who was "wild with joy at the freedom." In August, she and Anna changed places. There was no home life in Concord, for there was a constant turnover of strangers coming in as nurses. September found the family all together at Anna's house, and Anna and Louisa worn out.

In October it was back to Boston, first to the Bellevue, then to 31 Chestnut Street with John and Fred. Both the Pratt boys had "gone to business," John at Chase's Art Gallery and Fred as a reporter. Louisa began again on *Jo's Boys*.

"Wrote two hours for three days, then had a violent attack of vertigo & was ill for a week. Head wont bear work yet. Put away papers & tried to dawdle & go about as other people do. . . . Last day of the year. All well at home except myself," Louisa wrote. "Body feeble but soul improving."

Boston was very cold the winter of 1885. Louisa attended the opera and bought John his first dress suit, just as she had done for Fred. He would be twenty in June. Lulu was living with Anna, but she spent a week with Louisa in January.

Louisa was not well. She exchanged visits, and went about her social work, visiting the Blind Asylum and the North End Mission. But the vertigo, and the pains in her joints, and what she called her "nerves" were getting worse. In January she conquered her doubts and began a series of "Mind Cure" sessions with a Mrs. Newman. These were apparently a mixture of Christian Science (Bronson had been very interested in Mary Baker Eddy's theories) and hypnotism. Louisa found the experience pleasant at first ("Blue clouds & sunshine in my head"), but then her heart began to flutter and her breath grew short. She seemed to float away. She couldn't move. Hypnotism, Louisa concluded, although Mrs. Newman assured her it was not. In spite of her doubts, she resolved to continue the experiment in hope of some miracle, however small.

Her journal changed, becoming a kind of daily calendar of jottings—weather, activities, her health—all in short, choppy phrases. The Mind Cure was not a success, even though it was becoming very popular. Eventually, the Christian Science Church had to make clear that Mrs. Newman was not

Norma Johnston

31 CHESTNUT STREET, BOSTON. THIS HOUSE, WHERE LOUISA
MAY ALCOTT LIVED WITH HER NEPHEWS IN 1884, IS TYPICAL
OF HER BEACON HILL HOMES.

one of its practitioners. Louisa's health was deteriorating rapidly. Her eyes were giving her trouble, and her head ached constantly. The vertigo would attack for ten days at a stretch. Louisa began seeing Dr. Conrad Wesselhoeft fairly regularly. She had given up on Mrs. Newman after thirty sessions, and she would try no more "miracle cures." "My ills are not imaginary, so are hard to cure," she wrote.

One of her worst troubles was that her voice had failed her. Louisa had been plagued with coughs for years; now her voice alternated between hoarse and nonexistent. In spite of it all she was able to write, when she went home to Concord in April, "On the whole a good winter. . . . Sorry not to be better. Voice gone, head bad, & spirits low, being tired of the long fight for health. The hospital experience was a costly one for me. Never well since. Yet it turned the tide & brought success." "It" was *Hospital Sketches,* which had been her first literary and financial success. Louisa was a true daughter of the Mays, who could look back at the days and nights of the Union Hotel Hospital and see good coming out of all the sorrow and the horror. But Louisa had been right when she had written that she had broken the laws of health. She would never be well again.

She tried one treatment after another, the best modern medical science could suggest and her hard-earned money could buy. Oxygen . . . drug inhalation . . . morphine . . . "Pipe" (possibly opium). Neither the doctor nor Louisa knew that these drugs were addictive. They made her light-headed, and drug-dependent. They did not make her well. It was too late, and the causes and cures of her ill health were not known in 1885.

She went on, from Concord to Boston to Nonquitt and back to Concord. Lulu and family and pain and attempts to write. Louisa had become an old woman in everything except her mind. She could still identify with and appreciate the young.

She began going through her old letters, papers, and journals, editing them, destroying what she would not want the public to read. She decided it was time to uproot the whole family from Concord. It would be easier to care for Bronson in the city. She found a house at 10 Louisburg Square, the most fashionable block in the most fashionable part of Boston, and rented it for two years. Lulu could play in the iron-railed private park in the center of the square and enjoy the sight of all the Boston cats roosting on the statues of Aristides and Columbus.

Before the Alcotts moved, Concord celebrated its 250th anniversary. There was a great rally, a dinner, and a reception, with the governor himself in attendance. James Russell Lowell spoke. "Outsiders asked why Miss A was never invited to sit among the honored ones at such times? C[oncord] cant forgive her for not thinking it perfect," Louisa wrote bluntly.

There was a hard week of moving, for the house was not in good condition as promised. The family came later. Bronson was carried up to his new room and seemed pleased with it. Lulu was enchanted. Louisa knew this extended household meant the end of her Boston peace and quiet, but she knew that it was right. She could afford it; her books had never sold so well and she had started a collection of short stories called *Lulu's Library*.

She still hadn't gotten far on *Jo's Boys*.

The year 1886 came in, hard and cold. Louisa began a treatment of massages by her friend Dr. Rhoda Lawrence, who had been a model for a character in *Jack and Jill*. She reread *Eight Cousins* and liked it, and hoped that she was getting better.

By the end of February the dizzy spells began again. Louisa lay in bed, helpless and discouraged. She improved a little by Anna's birthday and gave her a $1,000 bond. She put the same sum in the bank for each of the boys. And she tried to write. Another attack of vertigo followed. "Ill for a week. Sleepless nights. Head worked like a steam engine & would not stop. Planned 'Jo's Boys' to the end & longed to get up & write it." She told Dr. Wesselhoeft, her consulting physician, that he had better let her get the ideas out of her head and onto paper; maybe then she could rest. He let her try for half an hour a day.

A week later Louisa collapsed. The cycle began again. Vertigo, racing brain, weakness . . . then sitting up, getting up, going out. By April she was writing for an hour or two a day. In June they all went back to Anna's house in Concord, and in July Louisa sent Anna and Lulu off to Nonquitt. She stayed in Concord with Bronson, and wrote.

Louisa was feeling well for the first time in months, perhaps in years. She finished *Jo's Boys* and corked her inkstand, but plots for more books were running through her head. The School of Philosophy opened, with Bronson in attendance. For Louisa the good times lasted all through the summer, but the first sign of warning came in late August. "Liver out of order," she noted. It wasn't her liver (a diagnosis given to all sorts of digestive problems at that time), but it *was* serious trouble, possibly cancer.

The trouble came on slowly, concealed partly by all Louisa's other ailments. Her head was bad, her cough was bad, she was dizzy. But bit by bit it was becoming impossible for her to digest food.

By December 18, Louisa was in such pain that she sought

refuge at the one place she thought she might find it—Dr. Rhoda Lawrence's nursing home on Dunreath Place in Roxbury, a Boston suburb.

"Saint's Rest," Louisa wrote at the head of her new journal for 1887. "A sad & lonely day. Feeble & sick, away from home & worn out with the long struggle for health. . . . Say my prayers & try to see many mercies. Fred & his happy love, A & her pride in her good boys, Lulu well & good & happy. Father comfortable, & plenty to make all safe & easy. More courage & patience are all *I* ask."

Fred was engaged to marry Jessica Cate, and Louisa rejoiced in their happiness. She was very weak and was being treated with *nux vomica,* which contained strychnine and could be a deadly poison. She was also getting injections. Her stomach problems had become much worse, and she was having nightmares and fearing for her sanity. Louisa's journal became an invalid's record, but the letters she wrote were still the old Louisa, able to find the dark humor in everything, even pain. At times she was able to leave the nursing home and return to Louisburg Square, where she read, wrote, sewed, went shopping, and enjoyed her Lulu.

Her legs were troubling her again. Her heart kept fluttering. Louisa rested grimly and then kept on going. She was putting her affairs in order. Thomas Niles wanted to reissue *A Modern Mephistopheles,* this time giving the author's name. Louisa said yes.

By summer she was surviving on gruel, beef juice, and massage, and she was losing weight. Louisa was concerned about what would happen to her copyrights if she died, for her books continued to earn money for the family. Someone suggested that she adopt John Pratt as her legal son. Anna was willing, John was willing, and Louisa was overjoyed. On June 27, three days after John's twenty-second birthday, the adoption went through. Louisa wrote to him, signing her letter, "Bless you, my son, yr MUM."

She had made her will. Everyone was provided for, including Lulu. Only Bronson remained as a burden on her mind. Other than that, Louisa was at peace, and she rallied to spend the summer quietly in Princeton. John came to visit, and so did Fred, bringing his Jessie.

That autumn, *Lulu's Library* and another short-story collection, *A Garland for Girls,* were published. By that time, Louisa was so sick she felt sure she was dying. She was back at Dunreath Place, this time for good. Her doctors tried one medicine after another, one treatment after another. Louisa still could not digest food, and her weight was falling alarmingly. Her legs and her head were in constant pain. "A hard year, but over now," Louisa wrote on December 31. "Please God the next be happier for us all."

"A happy day," Louisa wrote in her new journal on New Year's Day, 1888. "[T]hough still alone & absent from home I am on the road to health at last."

Louisa was getting better in the way of chronic invalids who are in remission: two steps forward and one step back. She had learned to be patient, but she longed to have a life again. What she wanted most was to attend Fred and Jessie's wedding in February, but she was far too weak. But Anna kept her up to date on all the details, and Louisa could write to friends and relatives about Jessie's heavy white corded silk wedding dress with pearl embroidery and Fred's new suit and white brocade vest. "She will look like a rose, & F. will be a landscape," Louisa wrote Laura Hosmer.

Two days after the wedding Louisa was called to Boston to Bronson's bedside. He was failing fast, and no one expected him to live. But he did. Louisa saw him again two days later, and two days after that, and three days more. Astonishingly, she herself was feeling better, enough so to attend to business, sew a little, and do some writing. She visited Fred and Jessie and saw their wedding presents.

Spring was coming. It would be Bronson's last spring, Louisa knew. He was ready to "go up," and she could not blame him. All the giants of his world were there already: Emerson. Thoreau. Margaret Fuller. Lyman Beecher. And Abba, his "dear Friend," "dear A!"

Louisa, too, had so many "dear ones" on the other side. Henry David Thoreau and Mr. Emerson, her first loves. John Pratt, friend and brother. May. "Marmee." Elizabeth.

She had done everything she had vowed to do long before, when she had sworn to make for Abba a quiet room, when Abba had given her a pen-case and bid her write.

She had given Father his one perfect school. She had provided art lessons and Europe for May; comforts for Abba's last years. She had made them all secure: Mother, Father, Anna, May, Lulu, and the boys. As for herself, she had lived many different lives, written many books and stories and become famous; she had had her silk dresses, her grand tour, and proper May homes on Beacon Hill.

"Bear your burdens gladly," Louisa had learned from *Pilgrim's Progress*. She had borne hers, if not always gladly, at least without ever losing her sense of humor. And the Celestial City glittered ever nearer in the eternal sun.

The only burden left was Father, and that would not be for long. On March 1 Louisa put on her outdoor clothes, wrapped herself in furs, and was driven to Louisburg Square for what both knew would be their last meeting. She found him childlike and serene, gazing at the ceiling. "I am going up. Come soon," he murmured as she knelt beside his bed.

"Oh, I wish I could," Louisa answered ruefully. That was not literally true. Louisa did not long to die, but she was not afraid of death. She longed to be done with pain, with weariness, with her inability to eat.

After she left Bronson's bedside, she and Anna sat together briefly, talking quietly. Then she went out into the March winds of Boston, lost in her thoughts, forgetting to put on her furs.

By evening she was feverish. Pneumonia, called "the old man's friend" because it meant an easy death, was setting in. She sank into unconsciousness, rousing only to recognize John and Dr. Rhoda Lawrence. Then the shadows swallowed her again.

For two days she lingered, not knowing Anna and the others were near. She died on March 6, 1888, at 3:30 A.M., never having been told that Bronson had "gone up" two days before. Perhaps she knew; perhaps that was why she was able at last to stop keeping on.

In *Little Women,* Louisa May had written:

> Oh, when these hidden stores of ours
> Lie open to the Father's sight,
> May they be rich in golden hours,
> Deeds that show fairer for the light.
> Lives whose brave music long shall ring
> With a spirit-stirring strain,
> Souls that shall gladly soar and sing
> In the long sunlight after rain.

Her life had indeed been "brave music," and it still rings.

BOOKS FOR FURTHER READING

Bedell, Madelon. *The Alcotts: Biography of a Family*. New York, NY: Clarkson N. Potter, Inc., 1980. A fascinating account of the lives of Bronson and Abba May Alcott, their families and their daughters, up to the time when Louisa May Alcott was twenty-one.

Cheney, Ednah D. *Louisa May Alcott: Her Life, Letters and Journals*. New York, NY: Chelsea House, 1981. The first biography of Louisa May Alcott, written (and the letters and journals considerably edited) by a close personal friend.

Elbert, Sarah. *A Hunger for Home: Louisa May Alcott's Place in American Culture*. New Brunswick, NJ: Rutgers University Press, 1987. A study of Louisa May Alcott's life and works in their historical context.

———, ed., Louisa May Alcott. *Moods*. New Brunswick, NJ: Rutgers University Press, 1991. 1864 edition, plus appendix, which contains Alcott's revisions for the 1882 edition, edited and with introduction by Sarah Elbert.

Meigs, Cornelia. *Invincible Louisa*. Boston, MA: Little, Brown & Co., 1933. A Newbery Award-winning biography of Louisa May Alcott.

Myerson, Joel, and **Daniel Shealy,** editors, and **Madeleine B. Stern,** associate editor. *The Selected Letters of Louisa May Alcott*. Boston, MA: Little, Brown & Co., 1987.

———. *The Journals of Louisa May Alcott*. Boston, MA: Little, Brown & Co., 1989.

Louisa May Alcott in her own words, the letters meant for her family, friends, fans, and business associates; the journals for her own (and her mother's) eyes only. Read together, they show her real courage and sense of humor; read along with *Little Women* and its sequels, they show how much Alcott drew on her own life for her novels. Each volume has a biographical introduction by Alcott scholar Madeleine B. Stern that fills in details Alcott herself omitted (or, in the case of her journals, destroyed). Both have the same useful year-by-year chronology of the Alcott family's lives, works, and homes.

Shealy, Daniel, Madeleine B. Stern, and **Joel Myerson.** *Louisa May Alcott: Selected Fiction*. Boston, MA: Little, Brown & Co., 1991. Samples of all types of fiction by Louisa May Alcott, from her early writing days on, including two newly discovered thrillers and excerpts from novels.

Shepard, Odell. *Pedlar's Progress: The Life of Bronson Alcott.* Westport, CT: Greenwood Press, 1968. A biography of Louisa May Alcott's father by the 1938 editor of his journals.

————. *The Journals of Bronson Alcott.* Boston, MA: Little, Brown & Co., 1938. Selections from Bronson Alcott's many journals edited by his biographer.

Stern, Madeleine B. *Louisa May Alcott.* Norman, OK: University of Oklahoma Press, 1950. The first of the modern biographies of Louisa May Alcott, by the feminist scholar who was later responsible for the editing and republication of Louisa May Alcott's "lost thrillers."

THE BOOKS OF LOUISA MAY ALCOTT

Louisa May Alcott wrote hundreds of books, articles, and stories, some under her own name, many under pseudonyms. Her best-known works are listed below. Your librarian can help you find out which are now in print and from which publishers. The out-of-print books can often be found at secondhand bookstores and garage or rummage sales.

For All Ages

Little Women (1868–1869)
An Old-Fashioned Girl (1870)
Little Men (1871)
Eight Cousins (1875)
Rose in Bloom (1876)
Under the Lilacs (1876)
Jack and Jill (1880)
Jo's Boys (1886)

For Adults

Hospital Sketches (1863)
Moods (1864)
Work: A Story of Experience (1873)

Short Stories (Collections)

Aunt Jo's Scrap Bag (1872)
Flower Fables (1855)
A Garland for Girls (1888)
Lulu's Library (1886–89)

Recent Publications
(Collections)

Behind a Mask: Unknown Thrillers by Louisa May Alcott. Madeleine B. Stern, ed. New York, NY: Wm. Morrow & Co., Inc., 1975.

A Double Life: Newly Discovered Thrillers of Louisa May Alcott. Madeleine B. Stern, Editor; Joel Myerson and Daniel Shealy, associate editors. Boston, MA: Little, Brown & Co., 1988.

Freaks of Genius: Unknown Thrillers of Louisa May Alcott. Daniel Shealy, editor; Madeleine B. Stern and Joel Myerson, associate editors. Westport, CT: Greenwood Press, 1991.

Louisa May Alcott: Selected Fiction. Edited by Daniel Shealy, Madeleine B. Stern, and Joel Myerson. Boston, MA: Little, Brown & Co., 1991.

Plots and Counterplots: More Unknown Thrillers of Louisa May Alcott. Madeleine B. Stern, editor. New York, NY: Wm. Morrow & Co., Inc., 1976.

ACKNOWLEDGMENTS

Permission to reprint excerpted material is gratefully acknowledged to the following:

Columbia University Press, for permission to quote from *The Letters of Ralph Waldo Emerson*, copyright © 1939.

Houghton Library, Harvard University, for permission to quote from the letters and diaries of Abba May Alcott, and the journals and diaries of Amos Bronson Alcott.

Iowa State University Press, for permission to quote from *The Letters of Amos Bronson Alcott*, R. L. Herrnstadt, editor, copyright © 1969.

Little, Brown and Company, for permission to quote from *The Selected Letters of Louisa May Alcott*, edited by Joel Myerson, Daniel Shealy, and Madeleine B. Stern. Compilation and narrative text copyright © 1987 by Joel Myerson, Daniel Shealy, and Madeleine B. Stern. Letters of Louisa May Alcott copyright © 1987 by the estate of Theresa W. Pratt.

And for permission to quote from *The Journals of Louisa May Alcott*, edited by Joel Myerson, Daniel Shealy, and Madeleine B. Stern. Compilation and narrative text copyright © 1989 by Joel Myerson, Daniel Shealy, and Madeleine B. Stern. Journals of Louisa May Alcott copyright © 1989 by the estate of Theresa W. Pratt.

The New York Public Library, Henry W. and Albert A. Berg Collection, and Astor, Lenox, and Tilden Foundations, for permission to quote from letter of Elizabeth Peabody to Mary Peabody and the Elizabeth Peabody holograph journal.

All photographs of the Alcott family are reproduced courtesy of the Louisa May Alcott Memorial Association.

INDEX

AAP   Anna Alcott Pratt
ABA   Amos Bronson Alcott
AMA   Abba May Alcott
ESA   Elizabeth Sewall Alcott
FAP   Frederick Alcott Pratt
JBP   John Bridge Pratt
JM   Col. Joseph May
JSP   John Sewall Pratt
LMA   Louisa May Alcott
LMN   Louisa May Nieriker
MAN   May Alcott Nieriker
RWE   Ralph Waldo Emerson
SJM   Rev. Samuel J. May, Jr.

Abolitionists, 21, 103–106

Alcott, Abba May, 140, 162–163
as abolitionist, 92; adolescence, 14; and
ABA, 199 (courtship, 17–19, 20–24;
disillusion in ABA, 51–52; engagement,
24–27; feelings toward ABA, 11, 16–18,
20–21, 24–25, 29, 34, 71, 92, 102–103;
leaves ABA, 60, 71; marital problems,
53–54, 60, 68–70, 71–72, 73–75, 90, 92–
93; meets ABA, 11, 16–18; reconcilia-
tions with ABA, 60, 93, 102–103;
wedding, 27); and ESA. See ESA; and
LMA, 74–75, 80–81, 95, 106–107, 137,
151–152, 158, 167, 172, 177–178, 194, 197,
199–200, 202–203, 224. See also LMA;
appearance, 12, 14, 16, 27, 98, 102–103,
162, 163; background, 12–14; characteristics, 12–19, 24, 26, 31, 44, 54–55, 71, 77,
84, 87, 89, 98, 133, 138; childbirths, mis-
carriages, pregnancies, 29, 30, 32, 38,
44–45, 47, 50; childhood, 14; death of,
200; education, 14; and RWE, 53; feminist, 92; financial support of family, 52,
54, 70, 76–77, 84, 98, 100. See also AMA,
money, occupations; and Fruitlands.
See Fruitlands; and grandchildren. See
FAP, JSP; as homemaker, 29, 127, 137;
illnesses, 32, 45, 90, 126, 137, 158, 162–163,
177, 194–195, 199; journals, 17–19, 24, 66;
and Lane, Charles, 68–71; and JM, 13,
44, 46; and May, Mary Cary, 15, 46;
and SJM, 11, 15–16, 24–25, 57, 69, 74;
and money, 26, 29, 51–52, 74, 76–78, 95,
97–98; and MAN, 50–51, 178, 200; occupations, 52, 83–84, 86–91, 100, 112–
113, 171, 184–185; in old age, 158, 162–163,
167, 174, 177–178, 191, 194–195, 197, 199–

200; and Peabody, Elizabeth, 36, 40,
44; and AAP, 29, 156, 178, 181, 198–199.
See also AAP; values, 29, 98, 133, 137

Alcott, Amos Bronson, x, xi, 1, 2
and abolition, 31, 103–106; adolescence,
5–8; appearance, 5, 16–17, 58, 77, 102–
103, 105, 149, 162–163; and AMA, 17–19,
20–21, 24–25, 29, 52, 93, 102–103, 177–
178, 199, 202–203, 215, 224. See also
AMA; and ESA, 38–45, 120–123; and
LMA, 30–31, 149, 151–152, 166, 184, 193,
196, 213, 223–225. See also LMA; and Alcox, Anna Bronson. See Alcox; and Alcox, Joseph. See Alcox; and Alcox,
Junius. See Alcox; background, 1–3; as
caregiver, 45, 149–152; characteristics, 1,
4–6, 8–10, 16–17, 24–26, 30, 44–45, 56,
65–66, 75, 88–89, 100, 103–105; childhood, 3–5; children, attitude toward, x,
28–29, 37, 133; and Concord, 83, 127, 181,
204, 206, 214–215, 220–221, 224; and
Consociate Family. See Consociate
Family; Fruitlands; and death, preoc-
cupation with, 69, 89; education, 3–5;
and RWE, 39, 45, 48, 56, 78, 97–98, 101–
102. See also RWE; and Fruitlands. See
Fruitlands; illnesses, mental and physical, 7, 24, 75, 88–89, 90, 100, 215; income, 7–8, 98, 102, 115, 137, 191; and
insanity, 177, 182. See also ABA, illnesses;
Alcox, Junius; journals, 4–5, 7, 17, 24,
47; and Lane, Charles, 60, 62–71, 73–
76; and Little Women, 184; marriage,
attitude toward, 41; and JM, 28, 44, 47,
129; and SMJ, 10–11, 17–18. See also SJM;
and money, 8, 25–26, 28–29, 43–44, 47–
49, 51–52, 78, 83, 90, 97–98, 181, 185; and
MAN, 50–51, 210. See also MAN; obses-
sive relationships, 71–75, 92–93; occupations (author, 28, 41–43, 45, 51, 55, 88–
89, 167, 177, 197, 215; "Conversations,"
45, 87, 89, 100, 137, 152; craftsman/
designer, 78, 127–128; educational theo-
rist, 9–10, 19, 28, 31, 37, 39, 46, 190;
farmer-gardener, 49, 78, 127–128, 133,
168; "ministry of talking," 45, 66–
68, 69–70, 84–85, 101–102, 113, 115, 117,
120, 162–163, 179, 181, 184, 191, 213, 215;
peddler, 6–9, 100–102; philosopher/
preacher, 31, 100, 130, 167–168, 204, 206,
215; psychologist, 28–29, 31, 33–35, 37,

45; schoolmaster/teacher, 6, 9–10, 19, 21–22, 25–26, 29–31, 37, 39, 40–41, 46, 47–48, 83, 127, 204); in old age, 192, 194–195, 204, 206, 210, 215, 216, 220; as parent, ix, 1, 33–35, 37, 51, 65; and Peabody, Elizabeth, 32, 40, 42; philosophical beliefs of, 6, 9, 59; and AAP, 29, 30, 33–35, 178, 214. *See also* AAP; and JBP. *See* JBP; pulled between two selves, 5–6, 24, 88–89; religion and ritual, 6, 8, 30, 38, 40–41, 65; and Temple School. *See* Temple School; and Thoreau, Henry David. *See* Thoreau; travels of, 7–8, 56–57, 102–103, 117, 162–163, 179, 181, 184, 194, 196; vegetarianism, 39–40, 59; whispering campaigns against, 9–10, 21, 24, 42; and women, 89, 92–93. *See also* AMA

Alcott, Elizabeth Sewall
    appearance, 38, 123, 151; and AMA, 38, 112–113, 116–120; and ABA, 38–45, 117, 120; and LMA, 117–121, 183, 225. *See also* LMA; birthdays, 38; birthdays, 50, 57–58, 65, 76–77, 113; characteristics, 8, 77, 117, 122; death of, 120–123, 145; education of, 87, 89; illnesses of, 90, 112–113, 115–120, 172; infancy and childhood of, 38, 45, 49–50; name changed, 44; occupations of, 70, 89; religious beliefs of, 121

Alcott, Louisa May
    and abolition, 98; as actress and producer/director, 50, 77, 82–83, 85, 88, 100, 109–111, 117–120, 124–126, 156, 166–167, 174, 204; adolescence, 70–78, 81, 85; adopts JSP, 222–223; and AMA, 74–75, 78–81, 95, 106–107, 137, 151–152, 158, 167, 169, 172, 177–178, 199–203, 214, 224 (as AMA's caregiver, 126–127, 137, 162–163, 167, 174, 177, 194, 197, 199); and ABA, 31, 34–35, 74–75, 80–81, 110–111, 114, 149–152, 166, 169, 184, 190, 193, 195, 203, 205–206, 212, 214, 223–225, (as ABA's caregiver, 193, 215, 220, 223); and ESA, 38, 117–124 (as ESA's caregiver, 113, 117–120; death of ESA, 120–123, 145, 178–179); and Alcott family, 153, 167, 194, 202, 216, 224; "Alcott Sinking Fund," 100, 132, 153, 185; appearance, 12, 30–31, 54, 77, 138, 147, 151–152, 156, 191, 204; as author, 75, 77, 80, 82, 93, 95–96, 100, 106–107, 109–113, 115–116, 126–127, 130, 132–133, 136–142, 146–147, 153–154, 156–159, 162–164, 166–178, 181–183, 187, 190–

191, 193, 195, 197–198, 204, 206–207, 214–216, 219–221, 223; birth, 28, 30; birthdays, 39, 74, 114, 126, 179, 187–188, 192; and Boston, 110–113, 124, 159, 165–166, 180–183, 191, 193, 195, 197–198, 204, 207, 210, 212–213, 224; as celebrity, 154, 156, 158, 174, 178, 180, 182–186, 190–196, 204, 206, 213, 224; characteristics, 31, 77, 95, 108, 202, 219, 220 (dedication to family, 78, 80, 202, 224; impatience, 160, 223; independence, 212; introspection, 54, 126, 160; jealousy, 38–39; loneliness, 87–88, 202–203; "May characteristics," 31, 80–81, 191, 206, 219; moods, 77, 80–81, 125–126, 140, 160–161, 187–188; "owling about," 160–161; power of observation, 54, 129; pride, 140–141, 160, 183; rebelliousness, 35; sense of humor, 114, 133, 158, 170, 182–184, 195, 204–205, 222; stubbornness, 206, 212; temper, 181; as tomboy, 40, 49–50, 62, 65; values, 111, 125, 129, 141, 153, 170, 178–179, 183, 192, 194, 198, 205, 219, 224); childhood, 40, 49–54, 60, 65–70, 133; Christmases, 114–115, 126, 137, 189, 190, 192, 196. *See also* Alcott celebrations and rituals; as city person, 129, 182–183. *See also* LMA and Boston; and Civil War. *See* Civil War; LMA and Union Hotel Hospital; clothing and style, 64, 100, 109–111, 114–115, 132–133, 137–138, 143–144, 151, 154, 156, 183–186, 191, 196, 214–215, 224–225; and Concord, 124, 129, 154, 167, 170, 180–182, 190–193, 196, 198, 205, 210, 212–213, 215–216, 219–221; cultural activities. *See* LMA, social life; death of, 223–225; at Dedham, MA, 94–95, 102, 195; drug dependency, 149, 186–187, 191, 205, 219; education, 34, 49, 76; and Emerson, Ellen, 85; and RWE, 50, 81–82, 85, 115, 136; as family housekeeper, 87–89, 94–95, 102, 153, 156, 180, 197, 216; fears, 74–75, 181–182, 203, 222; as feminist, 78, 176, 182, 184–185, 192, 206, 213; as financial support of family, 79–80, 85, 100, 115, 126, 132, 153, 156, 162–164, 181, 185, 191–193, 198, 204, 212, 216, 221–224. *See also* LMA and money; "Alcott Sinking Fund"; as foster mother, 212–213, 216. *See also* LAN; JSP; and Fruitlands, 65–76, 94; illnesses, 138, 150–153, 158, 160, 162–163, 186, 188, 190–195, 198–199, 202–207, 210, 214, 216–217, 219, (cough [bronchitis], 74, 147–149, 163, 167, 180–

234

181, 184, 219–221; delirium and fever,
147–151, 225; headaches, 180–181, 217,
219, 221, 223; mercury poisoning, 186–
187, 205–206, 222; pneumonia, 225;
rheumatism, 74, 163, 184, 186, 191, 205–
206, 217; smallpox, 90; stomach trouble, 221–223; typhus, 147–152; vertigo,
217, 219, 221); income, 94–96, 98, 100,
108–109, 112–113, 115, 125–126, 136–138,
144, 146, 152–153, 156, 158–159, 161–164,
166, 174, 180, 183, 190–195); journals, 66,
68–70, 74–76, 78, 80, 92, 94, 108, 117,
121–122, 126, 130, 133, 138, 140–142, 145,
147, 157–158, 162–163, 176, 178–180, 186,
190, 192–193, 195, 197, 199, 205–206, 212,
214–217, 219–223; and Kane, Dr.
William, 186–187; lifestyle, 129, 165–166,
191–193, 214, 220, 222, 224; and Little
Women, 164–172, 178, 180, 182; marriage, views on, 129, 167, 176, 182, 184–
185, 197; and JM, 46, 50, 171; and SJM,
163–164; and May family, 60, 110, 113,
170, 171, 181; and money, 54, 87–88, 108–
110, 113, 127, 132–133, 162, 164, 174, 181,
185, 192–195, 198, 219–224; and MAN,
50, 150, 152, 157, 167, 183, 185–186, 189–90,
192, 197, 202–204, 207, 210; as MAM's
mentor, 114, 124, 137, 156, 166, 181, 183,
190, 194; and LAN, 207, 210–214, 216–
217, 222; nightmares, 52, 181–182, 222;
occupations, 79, 108 (author. See LMA
as author; book reviewer, 111; companion, 94–95; editor, 32, 156, 164, 166–167,
181, 193; governess/tutor, 94, 109, 113, 115,
125, 129; housekeeper, 87–89, 94–95,
102; journalist, 82, 164–167, 193; lecturer, 192; nurse, 126–127, 129, 142, 144–
147, 149, 158, 199; seamstress/designer,
70, 89, 100, 109–113, 125, 132–133, 137–139,
153, 158, 167; schoolteacher, 83, 87, 89,
100–102, 115, 140–141, 190); and AAP,
112, 115–116, 123, 132, 137, 152–153, 167, 189,
194, 203–205, 216, 221–223, 225; and JSP,
162, 190, 294, 212, 215–217, 221–223; and
JBP, 140, 162, 185, 188–189, 224; and
FAP, 191, 212, 215–217, 221–224; pseudonyms, 93, 96, 154, 157–158, 182, 198; public service, 192, 204, 206, 217; religious
beliefs, 78, 80, 113, 126, 193, 225; romances and suitors, 50, 81, 94–95, 176–
177, 186–187, 198; "room of her own,"
79; saluted by Concord Militia, 154, 156;
and slaves/slavery, 112, 131–132, 156–157,
192; social life, 108–110, 113–115, 124–127,

129, 132–133, 138, 157, 161–167, 179, 183–
184, 186–187, 192, 196, 204–206, 214, 217;
as social reformer, 184–185, 197, 206, 213;
sources of book material, 111–112, 116,
130, 132, 151, 160–161, 163, 167–174, 178,
181–187, 190, 193, 197, 203, 207, 220; spin-
sterhood, views on, 167, 176, 184–185;
and Temple School, 39, 172; and Thoreau, Henry David, 50, 81–82; travels,
115–116, 157, 159–164, 185–190, 195, 213–
214, 216, 219, 223, 224; and Union Hotel
Hospital, 142, 144–147, 180, 219; and her
"vortex," 127, 133, 137–138, 170, 172, 174,
176, 179, 181–182, 184, 193–194, 204; and
Wisniewski, Ladislas, 160–161. See also
"Lawrence, Laurie"; and Weld, Anna,
159–161; women, portrayal in LMA's
writing, 82–83, 112, 167, 184–185; and
women's rights, 78, 176, 182, 184–185,
192, 206; work style, 167, 169–170, 174,
179, 184, 191–192, 194–195, 197–199, 207,
216, 221. See also LMA, journals; LMA,
"vortex"

LMA: Works
Eight Cousins, 195, 197, 220; Flower
Fables, 106; Garland for Girls, A, 223;
"Happy Women," 167; Hospital
Sketches, 153–154, 174, 219; "An Hour,"
157–158; "How I Went Out to Ser-
vice," 102, 195; Jack and Jill, 207, 220;
Jo's Boys, 215, 217, 220–221; Little Men,
189–191, 195, 205; Little Women, ix,
176–178, 180, 182–185, 205, 207, 225;
"Love and Self-Love," 130; Lulu's Li-
brary, 220, 223; "Mark Field's Mis-
take," 127; "Mark Field's Success," 127;
"Masked Marriage, A," 96; "Modern
Cinderella, A," 132, 136; Modern Me-
phistopheles, A, 162, 222; Moods, 136, 137,
154, 157–159, 162, 170, 190, 214; "Mrs.
Jarley's Waxworks," 166; An Old-
Fashioned Girl, 182–185, 195, 197, 205;
"A Pair of Eyes," 140; "Pauline's Pas-
sion and Punishment," 146–147; "The
Rival Painters," 95–96, 100, 174; "The
Rival Prima Donnas," 106, 109, 111–
112; Rose in Bloom, 197; "Shawl Straps,"
193; Success. See Work; "Sunlight," 96;
"Sunshine," 93; "Transcendental Wild
Oats," 71; "Transfiguration," 203; Un-
der the Lilacs, 199; "A Whisper in the
Dark," 140; "With a Rose, That
Bloomed on the Day of John Brown's

Martyrdom," 130; *Work: A Story of Experience,* 138, 157, 194

Alcott Family
background, 1–4; celebrations and rituals, 39, 50, 57–58, 65, 75–77, 114–115, 132–133, 137, 139, 140, 158, 177–180, 185, 189, 192, 196, 199, 213, 216; family post office, 66, 70, 102; income. *See* ABA, AMA, LMA; lifestyle, 40, 50, 60, 64, 71–72, 100, 116, 127–128, 132–133, 191.

Alcott homes:
7 Allston St., Boston, 193; 88 Atkinson St., Boston, 90; Bath Spa Hotel, NYC, 196; 23 Beacon St., Boston, 91; Bedford St., Concord, 116; 6 Beech St., Boston, 46; Bellevue Hotel, Boston, 180, 196–198, 204, 207, 215, 217; "Brick Ends," Still River, 72; 26 E. Brookline St., Boston, 194; Charles St., Boston, 25; 34 Chauncy St., Boston, 113, 125; 53 Chauncy St., Boston, 181; 31 Chestnut St., Boston, 217; 98 Chestnut St., Boston, 110–111, 125; Cottage Place, Boston, 44; Dedham Place, Boston, 87; Dove Cottage, Concord, MA, 49, 56, 58–59; Dunreath Place, Roxbury, 221–225; East Boston, 163; Federal Court, Boston, 21, 171; 21 Federal St., Boston, 33; 26 Front St., Boston, 40; 44; Fruitlands, Harvard, MA, 65–76, 94, 147, 180; Germantown, 32; 12 Groton St., Boston, 89; 6 Hayward Place, Boston, 165; Hillside, Concord, 78, 84, 97–98, 116, 123, 170; 50 High St., Boston, 91; Hosmer Cottage, Concord, 49; Hosmer Farm, Concord, 77; 10 Louisburg Square, Boston, 220, 222; Lovejoy home, Still River, 76; Malden, 178; Nonquitt, 216, 219, 221; Orchard House, Concord, 116, 117, 120, 129, 132–133, 137, 150–151, 156, 158, 167–168, 170, 177–178, 190, 192, 200, 203, 206, 216; Philadelphia, 29; 20 Pinckney St., Boston, 98–100; 43 Pinckney St., Boston, 183; 81 Pinckney St., Boston, 212; The Pines, Germantown, 29; Spindle Hill, Wolcott, 2–5, 8, 10, 28, 71, 116, 193, 199; 1 Temple Place, Boston, 88; S. Third St., Philadelphia, 31; Thoreau House, Concord, 198–200; Walpole, 109, 112–113, 115–116; Wayside, Concord. *See* Hillside

Alcott House (England), 56–57, 64
"Alcott Sinking Fund", 100, 132, 153, 185

Alcox, Anna Bronson, 3, 47, 100–101, 116, 156
Alcox, Joseph Chatfield, 2
Alcox, Junius, 57–58, 89, 100–101
Alcox, William, 3, 11
Asylum for the Blind, 217
The Atlantic, 130, 132, 136, 137

Bane, Robert, 146–147
"Barnard, A. M.," 157, 198
Barry, Thomas R., 109, 111–112, 124
Bartlett, Alice, 185, 189–190
Bartlett, George, 177
Beacon Hill, 98, 100, 165, 220
Bellevue Hotel. *See* Alcott homes
"Bhaer, Professor," 179, 190
boardinghouses, 25, 29, 31, 33, 113, 125, 163, 181
Boston, MA, 12, 20–21, 86–89, 90–91, 103–106, 124, 129, 156, 159, 162, 165–166, 171, 183, 191, 197–198, 204, 213–214, 216, 219, 220
Boston *Commonwealth,* 153, 157
Boston *Recorder,* 9
Bower, Samuel, 63, 68
Bronson, Tillotson, 4, 5, 9, 10
Bronson family, 3
Brook Farm community, 63, 66, 171
"Brooke, John," 129–130, 137
Brown, John, 129–130, 137
   wife and children of, 133, 139
Burnett, Frances Hodgson, 205
Burns, Anthony, 103–106, 130

Calvinism, 2, 6, 21
Carnival of Authors, 204
"Celestial City," 5, 170, 224
Cheney, Ednah Littlehale, 39, 92–93, 101
Cheney, Seth, 93, 101
Cheshire Academy, 5, 10
Cheshire Primary School #1, 5–6, 9–10
child psychology, 29, 33–35
Christian Science, 217, 219
Christian Union, 193, 194
Civil War, 129–130, 138, 140–141, 143, 154, 157, 159, 174
Committee of Vigilance, 103–107
Concord, MA, 48, 83, 116, 124, 127, 129–130, 133, 136, 139, 141, 154, 156, 170, 172, 181–182, 191, 196, 198, 205–206, 210, 212–216, 219–221
Concord School of Philosophy, 204, 206, 214–215, 221

236

Congregationalism, 6
Consociate Family, 61, 62–72, 73–76, 87

Dickens, Charles, 110, 120, 126, 156, 165–166, 170
Dissenters, 2
Dix, Dorothea, 144, 149
Dodge, Mary Mapes, 195, 197, 199, 205, 207, 215
drugs, 187, 191, 219

Emerson, Edward, 139
Emerson, Ellen, 83, 85
Emerson, Ralph Waldo, 42, 52–53, 56, 58–59, 61, 65, 69, 81, 115, 123, 130, 132–133, 137, 153, 166, 171, 196, 214, 224; and LMA, 50, 81–82, 85, 136, 210; and ABA, 39, 43, 45, 48, 51, 56–57, 78, 97–98, 101–102, 210
Episcopalians, 6
Everett, Abraham, 63, 68

feminism. See AMA; LMA; women's rights movement
Field, J. M., 112
Fields, James T., 102
Fitzgerald, Richard, 146
French, Daniel Chester, 196
Frothingham, Samuel May, 14
Fruitlands, 61–76, 147, 180
Fugitive Slave Law, 91–92, 98–100, 103–106
Fuller, Margaret, 42–43, 51–52, 92

"Gamp, Sairy," 165–166
Gardner, Sophia, 76
Geist, Dr. Christian, 120, 123
Greaves, James Pierrepont, 55–57
Greele family, 24–25

Haines, Reuben, 29–30
Hancock, Dorothy Quincy, 13, 115, 171, 183
Hancock, John, 13
Hawthorne, Nathaniel, 58, 97, 123, 124, 157, 182
Hawthorne family, 58, 133, 142, 150
Hayden, Lewis, 104
Healy, George, 190
Higginson, Thomas Wentworth, 104–105, 178
Holmes, Oliver Wendell, 205
Hosmer family, 49, 66, 140, 206, 223
Howe, Julia Ward, 184
"Hummel family," 171

Huntington, Dr., 123
hypnotism, 217

The Independent, 193, 195

Kane, Dr. William, 186–187

Lane, Charles, 57–76, 83, 129
Lane, William, 58, 60, 74
Larned, Samuel, 63, 68
Lawrence, Dr. Rhoda, 205–206, 220–222, 225
"Lawrence, 'Laurie' (Theodore)," 160–161, 171, 179, 182, 203
"Lawrence, Mr.," 171
Leslie, Frank, 140–141, 146, 153, 157–159, 162, 166, 172
Lewis, Dr. Dio, 136, 180
Littlehale, Ednah Dow. See Cheney
Little Men. See LMA, Works
Little Women. See LMA, Little Women; LMA, Works
Lovering, Alice, 113, 115, 125
Lovering family, 115, 125–127
Lovejoy family, 66, 75, 76

"March, Amy," 168–169, 176, 178, 183, 203
"March, Aunt," 171, 190
"March, Beth," 168–169, 176, 178–179, 183, 203
"March, Jo," 168–172, 174, 176, 179, 183, 190
"March, Meg," 168–172, 176, 178, 183
"March, Mr.," 176
"March, Mrs. (Marmee)," ix, x, 167–169, 203
marriage in nineteenth century, 25. See also ABA, AMA, CL, LMA
Martineau, Harriet, 55
May, Catherine. See Windship
May, Dorothy Sewall, 13–15
May, Edward, 14
May, Elizabeth. See Willis
May, John, 12
May, Col. Joseph, 12–15, 25, 28, 46, 53, 171, 184–185
May, Joseph, 16
May, Louisa. See Greele
May, Lucretia Coffin, 11, 16, 25, 106, 110
May, Mary, 84
May, Mary Ann Cary, 15, 46
May, Rev. Samuel Joseph, 10–11, 13–14, 16, 48, 52, 55, 62, 74, 77, 106, 110, 123, 132, 163–164, 181, 191

May family, 12–14, 17–18, 48, 57, 60, 90, 109, 169, 171, 179
medicine in nineteenth century, 83, 90, 147, 149, 184, 186–187, 191, 216–217, 219, 222
Merry's Museum, 164, 174, 181–183
Miller, Dr. Eli Peck, 196
Mott, Lucretia, 31
"Mrs. Jarley's Waxworks," 106, 204

"New Eden," 57, 60–62, 170
"New Jerusalem," 21, 62, 86
New York Ledger, 167
Newman, Mrs., 217, 219
"Newness, The," 57–60
Nieriker, Ernest, 203, 210. *See also* LAN; MAN
Nieriker, Louisa May, 210–213, 215–217, 219–220, 222
Nieriker, Abba May Alcott, 50–51, 81, 132, 153, 166, 183, 191, 213, 225
and LMA, 114, 126, 137, 142, 153, 156, 166, 181, 183, 189–191, 194, 197, 200, 203–204, 207, 210, 225; appearance and characteristics, 50, 77, 152, 203; as artist, 114, 124, 133, 137, 151, 166, 174, 186–187, 195, 199, 203; as art student, 126–129; as art teacher, 137, 139–140, 166, 181, 196; childhood, 50, 51, 89; and Nieriker, Ernest, 203–204, 210; and Nieriker, Louisa May, 206; and parents, 50–51, 178
Nieriker, Sophy, 210–212
Nightingale, Florence, 144
Niles, Thomas, 164, 166–167, 172, 174–176, 180, 182, 190, 198, 202–203
"No Name Series," 198
Norris, Thomas, 95
nurses and nursing, 144. *See also* LMA occupations; Union Hotel Hospital

The Olive Branch, 95, 100, 174
"The Olive Leaf," 172
Orchard House. *See* Alcott homes; *Little Women*

Page, Ann, 66
"Palace Beautiful," 5
Palmer, Joseph, 64
"Paradise Lost," 4, 182
Parker, Rev. Theodore, 103–107, 114, 123, 125, 214
"Pathetic Family," 116
Peabody, Elizabeth, 32, 36–40, 42–44, 52, 55, 123, 132, 140–141

Peabody, Sophia, 42–43, 58
"Periwinkle, Tribulation," 154, 158, 182
Pickle Roost, 117, 124, 126, 192, 194, 197
Pickwick Club, 82, 172
Pilgrims, 2
Pilgrim's Progress, 4–5, 170, 224
Plato, 36
"Pottle, Widow," 124

Pratt, Anna Bronson Alcott, 84, 191, 195, 217, 221
as actress, 77, 117–120, 124; adolescence, 60, 64, 76–77. *See also* Fruitlands; appearance, 132, 205; and AMA, 29, 156, 178, 179–181; and ABA, 29–30, 214, 216; and ESA, 113, 117–120, 121–123; and LMA, 30, 31, 112, 130, 137, 150–153, 183, 189, 194–195, 204–205, 221, 223, 225; as Alcott housekeeper, 121, 197, 216; birth, 29; characteristics, 30–31, 35, 38, 68, 109–110, 113; childhood, 29–31, 33–35, 38, 48, 49–50, 53–54, 57–58, 60; deafness, 167; education, 50, 66, 76; as financial support of family, 100, 110, 113; illnesses, 112, 153, 157–158, 162, 194, 204, 216; and money, 100, 110, 113, 189, 198; occupations, 52, 89, 100, 106, 109–110, 113; and FAP, 152–153, 191, 195, 222; and JBP, 117–120, 124, (courtship and, 117–120, 124, 171, 172; married life, 137, 140, 163, 178; wedding, 132–133; widowhood, 188, 189;) and JSP, 159, 191, 195, 222; and Pratt family, 194, 197

Pratt, Frederick, Alcott, 153, 156, 158, 162–163, 178–179, 197, 212–214, 217, 222, 223
and LMA, 162, 167, 193, 204, 212, 215–216, 221, 223–224
Pratt, Jessica Cate, 222–224
Pratt, John Bridge, 123–124, 158, 162, 167, 170, 190–191, 225
and LMA, 130, 140, 162, 185. *See also* AAP
Pratt (Alcott), John Sewall, 159, 162–163, 178–179, 193, 197, 212–214, 217, 222
and LMA, 162, 167, 204, 212, 215, 221, 222–223
Pratt family, 132–133, 191, 194, 197
Princeton, MA, 223

Quakers, 29, 31, 196
Quincy, Dorothy. *See* Hancock, Dorothy Quincy
Quincy family, 13

Radical Club, 166, 179
Record of a School, 55
Redpath, James, 154, 156
Reed, Mr. & Mrs. David, 113, 125
Roberts Brothers, 154, 156, 164, 174, 177, 181, 184, 193–194, 197–198, 207
Robie, Hannah, 54, 84
Robinson, Susan, 48
Romanticism, 20–21
Ropes, Hannah, 142, 145, 147, 149
Russell family, 17–18, 29–30, 46

St. Nicholas, 195, 207
Sanborn, Franklin Benjamin, 117, 123, 130, 132, 139, 153, 156, 164
Saturday Evening Gazette, 106, 113
Savage, Mrs. James, 88
Sedgewick, Charles, and family, 106
Separatists, 2
Sewall family, 13, 40, 78, 90, 97–98, 110, 125, 150, 162, 181
Shadrach, 92, 103
Shakers, 76
Simms, Thomas, 103–104
slaves and slavery, 8, 21, 86, 92, 98–100, 103, 129–132, 156. *See also* abolition
Sleepy Hollow Cemetery, 121
"Slough of Despond," 5, 170
social-welfare movement. *See* AMA, occupations; LMA, public service; LMA as social reformer
Socrates, 33, 36, 43
Spindle Hill, 2–3, 8, 10, 28, 71
"The Spread Eagle," 174
Springfield *Republican,* 182
Stipp, Dr., 147–148
Stowe, Harriet Beecher, 98, 100, 192–193
Suhre, John, 146

Temple School, 33, 36–38, 43–44, 55, 126, 172
Thoreau, Henry David, 49–50, 58, 63, 123, 130, 132, 224
Thoreau House, 198

"Tetterby, Sophia," 117, 120
transcendentalism, 32
Tubman, Harriet, 133
Tuckerman, Salisbury, 126

Underground Railroad, 91, 98–100, 133
Uncle Tom's Cabin, 98–100
Union Hotel Hospital, 142, 144–147, 149, 180, 186, 219
Unitarianism, 13, 117
U.S. Sanitary Commission, 143–144, 152, 156

"Valley of Humiliation," 170
Vaux, Roberts, 30
vegetarianism, 39, 40, 59, 63
"vortex," 88–89. *See also* LMA, vortex

Waterford Cure House, 83–84
Wayside. *See* Alcott homes, Hillside
Weld, Anna and George, 159–161
Wells, Lizzie, 84, 110, 123, 152, 189, 212
Wesselhoeft, Dr. Conrad, 219, 221
Whitman, Alfred, 120, 125, 146, 171
Whitman, Walt, 113
The Wide, Wide World, 168
Willis, Elizabeth, 109
Willis, Elizabeth May, 14
Willis, Hamilton, 109, 114–115, 139
Willis, Llewellyn, 77, 82, 95, 146, 152
Willis, Louisa, 75, 109, 114–115, 126, 129, 139, 152
Windship, Catherine May, 14
Windship, Charles, 14, 26
Wisniewski, Ladislas, 160–161, 171
women, employment and salaries of. *See* AMA, occupations, income; LMA, occupations, income, money
women in Civil War, 144
women's rights movement, 92, 144, 179, 206
Wood, Abram, 63
Wright, Henry Gardiner, 57–59

The Youth's Companion, 166

MORE REAL-LIFE ADVENTURES
FROM BEECH TREE

E.B. White: Some Writer! by Beverly Gherman. E.B. White is known by millions as the creator of three children's classics—*Charlotte's Web, Stuart Little,* and *The Trumpet of the Swan.* Here is a chance for those who have treasured these novels to meet the man behind them. Illustrated with photographs.
(ISBN 0-688-12826-2; $4.95)

But I'll Be Back Again by Cynthia Rylant. In this moving autobiography, Newbery Award-winner Cynthia Rylant describes some of the most profound influences on her life: her grandmother, a tiny town called Beaver, the Beatles (especially Paul), and Robert Kennedy. Illustrated with photographs from the writer's personal collection.
(ISBN 0-688-12653-7; $4.95)

So Far from the Bamboo Grove by Yoko Kawashima Watkins. Though she is Japanese, eleven-year-old Yoko has always lived in Korea. But when the Second World War ends, Japanese on the peninsula are in danger. Yoko, her mother, and her sister must flee from their beautiful house with its peaceful bamboo grove. Their harrowing journey to safety forms the backbone of this remarkable story.
(ISBN 0-688-13115-8; $4.95)